Chain Reaction

A CALL TO
COMPASSIONATE REVOLUTION

Darrell Scott

THOMAS NELSON PUBLISHERS®
Nashville

Published in Nashville, Tennessee, by Thomas Nelson, Inc.

Scripture quotations are from THE NEW KING JAMES VERSION. Copyright © 1979, 1980, 1982, Thomas Nelson, Inc.

Scripture quotations noted NIV are from The Holy Bible: New International Version®. Copyright © 1973, 1978, 1984 by International Bible Society. Used by Permission of Zondervan Publishing House. All rights reserved.

ISBN 0-7852-6680-1

Printed in the United States of America.

5 6 – 06

Contents

This book is dedicated to Rachel Joy Scott.

May her memory remain alive through the chain reaction she started by acts of kindness.

Rachel, I love you.

Acknowledgments

Special thanks to my wife, Sandy, who has been an incredible support. Thanks to Steve Rabey, Wes Yoder, Tim Grable, Bob and Terry Cornuke, Paul and Nancy Cornuke, Josh and Dottie McDowell, Paul Jackson, Bob Mumford, Wayne and Betsy Worthy, John and Kimberly Curtis, John and Doreen Tomlin, Michael W. Smith, Bryan Boorujy, Gary and Billie Jean Bauer, Wes Cantrell, Tom Lang, Bruce Porter, Bill Epperhart, Dana Scott, Craig Scott, Mike Scott, Don and Bethanee McCandless, Buz and Nancy Hicks, my dad and mom, Grandma Kaye, Ryan Hollingshead, Cory Hollingshead, Tyler Hollingshead, all my friends at Thomas Nelson Publishers, all my friends at Ambassador Agency, and the millions of young people who will carry Rachel's legacy.

Be sure to check our Web site at: www.RachelScott.com

or

www.TheColumbineRedemption.com

v

Foreword

I met Darrell Scott for the first time while he was still freshly grieving over the loss of his beautiful daughter, Rachel Joy Scott, who was killed in the terrible tragedy at Columbine High School. Since that moment of tragedy we have developed a close personal relationship that has truly impacted my life.

Darrell has spoken to over a million people since I first met him, speaking continually in colleges, high schools, churches, football stadiums, civic centers, and arenas. The message he shares about his daughter's life and writings has positively changed the lives of countless young people around the world.

His message goes much farther and much deeper than just the Columbine tragedy. This book is Darrell's personal challenge to you and me, the reader, to start a chain reaction with our lives that affects the lives of those around us and beyond. It is a powerful challenge, based on his daughter's legacy, that offers new hope and purpose for your life.

Josh McDowell
Author and International
Youth Speaker

1
The Calm at the Center of the Storm

Merely mention the word *Columbine* in a conversation and the reaction you get demonstrates that the Denver area high school where my daughter and eleven other students and one teacher were killed has unfortunately become the most famous high school in the world.

A writer for *Time* magazine summarized the tragedy and its challenge to all of us:

> With each passing day of shock and grief you could almost hear the church bells tolling in the background, calling the country to a different debate, a careful conversation in which even presidents and anchormen behave as though they are in the presence of something bigger than they are.

Even people in Israel and Northern Ireland—regions of the world we think of as troubled hot spots—immediately associate the word *Columbine* with internationally televised images of the chaos and killing that erupted shortly before noon on April 20, 1999, when two angry and heavily armed students walked into the school and opened fire.

I realized how Columbine has become a symbol for tragedy around the world when I was in Iran in the summer of 2000. I had gone there with my friend Bob Cornuke and a team of adventurers to visit and research a mountain near the Turkish border. Part of the team included my dear friend John Tomlin, whose son was also killed that tragic day at Columbine.

We pitched our tents next to a nomad village high up on the mountainside. Sheep were everywhere and even some camels grazed nearby. I had our interpreter ask the teenage boys in the village if they had ever heard of the tragedy at Columbine, and to my amazement they all began to nod their heads. What really got to me, though, was that a couple of them had actually seen Rachel's funeral on CNN when they had visited the nearby city of Ardibil. Here I was in a nomad village thousands of miles from America talking to teenagers who knew about my daughter!

For me and for many of the people whose lives have been directly touched by the Columbine tragedy, the past two years have been something like living through a daily hurricane.

Internally, there has been a constant feeling of loss and grief about lives so full of promise that were indiscriminately snuffed out years before their time. Externally, there has been the storm of media coverage and the pain and turmoil resulting from ongoing investigations into the crime.

As in most tragedies of this kind there are, justifiably, numerous lawsuits that affect both innocent and guilty parties. There is the insidious toll on personal finances and relationships. There is the aftermath of myriad tortured memories that spring up at unexpected moments.

Two suicides in Columbine-area families that have been touched by the killings only add to the sorrow and serve as painful reminders of the bitter fruit that can result—sometimes many years later—from the destructive deeds that people do.

My son Craig was one of the people deeply affected by the tragedy. He saw his friends Matt Kechter and Isaiah Shoels murdered on either side of him as the three huddled together underneath a table in the Columbine library.

Craig's trauma from seeing his classmates killed would have been terrible enough, but he also has the memory of hearing the gunshots that killed his sister Rachel, who was sitting in the grass just outside the library walls. Craig's struggles to deal with all of this were partly documented and seen by millions of Americans during a broadcast on NBC's *Dateline*.

My purpose in writing this book isn't to wallow in the sorrows of the Columbine tragedy. Rather, this book reflects a radical hope and contains a challenge to everyone to see the hope that can often lie hidden beneath the horrors of life.

This book is a record of lessons learned during two difficult years, of calm found at the center of a storm, and of a hope-filled message about how each of us can help change our world into a place where fewer tragedies like Columbine happen.

A Memorial of Love

The Taj Mahal is a majestic building in northern India made of hundreds of tons of white marble and surrounded by gardens and pools.

Hailed as one of the wonders of the world, the Taj Mahal was built by some twenty thousand workers between 1632 and 1653.

This massive building wasn't constructed as a palace for its builder, the Indian ruler Shah Jahan. Rather, he erected it as a memorial for his beloved wife.

In a sense, this book is my Taj Mahal for Rachel. But the memorial I am building is not made out of marble and mortar. Rather, I'm remembering Rachel with this book by continuing her legacy and trying—like her—to positively impact the lives of other people.

A big part of my motivation is simply a father's desire to honor his daughter. However, another part of me realizes that good must triumph over evil, that Rachel's kindness must obliterate Eric's cruelty, that her chain reaction must go farther than his. Ironically, at times I feel that seeing my daughter's message bring the positive changes to so many others is my primary purpose in life.

Please don't misunderstand what I'm saying. I would have never chosen this as my life's calling. If I could bring Rachel back to live a full, productive life, I would. I would gladly stop writing and speaking and return to the peaceful anonymity I enjoyed before all this happened. But I can't reverse time. I can't pretend that Columbine never happened. I can grieve over the loss, but I can also rejoice in the powerful impact that her life has made in the lives of so many others. It was what she lived for, to make a positive difference in the lives she touched.

Chain Reaction: A Simple but Profound Message

Rachel committed her life to the belief that each person, by reaching out to others in compassion and kindness, could start a powerful chain reaction of goodness that just might change the world. This book attempts to convey the same message.

Rachel spelled out her beliefs in an essay she called "My Ethics, My Codes of Life." We'll take a closer look at the entire essay in a later chapter, but for now, let's look at a key passage that summarizes her approach:

> I have this theory that if one person can go out of their way to show compassion, then it will start a chain reaction of the same. People will never know how far a little kindness can go.

There are undoubtedly some people who don't think this kind of approach is worth very much in the push and shove of our "real" world. After all, Rachel was killed by two young men who set out to start a destructive and deadly chain reaction of their own (we'll talk about that in the next chapter).

But her death doesn't mean that she was wrong. People throughout history have died for the truth.

I agree with so many who expressed that Columbine was a "wake-up call for America." I believe that now is the time for us to actively bring about the changes that are needed so that our schools are once again the safe havens they once were.

Ours is a time when many people struggle with feelings of doubt and worthlessness. As a result they are too easily tempted to give in to feelings of selfishness, anger, and hatred. Others find it easier to do nothing about problems around them, or to spend hours losing themselves with video games or the Internet, rather than rolling up their sleeves and getting involved in the world and the lives of people around them.

As a result, every day millions of young Americans attend schools where one group of students bullies another and nobody does anything to stop it. And in many other cases, students are afraid that their school will be the next place where deadly violence will erupt. Instead of enjoying their youth and feeling safe in their schools, they are looking over their shoulders to see if someone is stalking them.

To some, things might look bad, but I think the opposite. Columbine remains a defining moment for many people, and Rachel's code of ethics contains part of the answer we need to create a better world. I believe there is no better time for hearing Rachel's message than the present.

A Defining Event

A number of newspapers and magazines have called Columbine a defining event for a generation. I think they might be right, but it's a sorrowful symbol for our time.

I'm in my fifties, and for people of my generation, one of the defining events of our lives was the assassination of President John F. Kennedy in 1963.

Not everyone had voted for Kennedy. In fact, the 1960 presidential race between Kennedy, a Democrat, and Republican Richard Nixon was one of the closest elections in American history—although not as close as the controversial 2000 race between George Bush and Al Gore.

Regardless, when Kennedy was gunned down, the nation stood still. Kennedy had been one of the youngest American presidents, and he had a beautiful wife and adorable young children. No matter how people felt about his politics or his policies, his death was a terrible tragedy.

In addition, the event was one of the first American news

events to be covered extensively by the relatively new technology of live television, and for days, Americans stayed glued to their TV sets as bizarre new details about the crime emerged.

Now decades later, people still visit the Dallas street where the killing took place, and every year hundreds of thousands of people visit a nearby museum, many of them wiping away tears of sadness as they examine the many displays explaining the turmoil of the 1960s or watch some of the video clips of the attractive young president in action.

Many people responded to the Kennedy assassination with despair and hopelessness, but amazingly, others found in its somber realities the inspiration to change the world by getting involved in America's growing Civil Rights movement or by going overseas to work with the Peace Corps.

For earlier generations, the Holocaust was a defining event. War has always been hellish, but no world leader had ever inflicted hell on people the way Hitler did in World War II. He scientifically and systematically rounded up, imprisoned, and killed millions of Jews and other innocent people, forcing the world to confront a whole new level of human atrocity.

But even this tragedy inspired some victims to try to live better lives. Victor E. Frankl was a psychiatrist in Austria when the Nazis invaded. Rounded up and sent off to Auschwitz concentration camp, Frankl became prisoner number 119,104 and was forced to adjust to a life of grinding hunger, bitter cold, horribly cramped conditions, relentless work, and constant misery as he watched many of his fellow prisoners become ill and die.

Such experiences turned some camp survivors into bitter pessimists, but Frankl emerged as an even more committed optimist. As he wrote in his 1945 book *Man's Search for Meaning,* "Life holds a potential meaning under any conditions, even the most miserable ones" (fourth edition, Beacon Press, 1992, p. 12).

Frankl's book, which many historians and critics consider one of the ten most influential books in America, is a powerful description of the horrors of the camps as well as the resilience of the human spirit. One of the book's central passages reveals Frankl's main message:

> The experiences of camp life show that man does have a choice of action. There were enough examples, often of a heroic nature, which proved that apathy could be overcome, irritability suppressed. Man *can* preserve a vestige of spiritual freedom of independence of mind, even in such terrible conditions of psychic and physical stress.
>
> We who lived in concentration camps can remember the men who walked through the huts comforting others, giving away their last piece of bread. They may have been few in number, but they offer sufficient proof that everything can be taken from a man but one thing: the last of the human freedoms—to choose one's attitude in any given set of circumstances, to choose one's own way. (pp. 74–75)

In a sense, this is what I have tried to do in the two years after the Columbine tragedy, and I am challenging others to do the same.

A Traumatic Topic

There had been school shootings before Columbine, but none of them was as deadly. None of the others generated round-the-clock TV coverage. None of the others spawned nearly a dozen books or countless songs and essays.

The *Denver Post* is one of two Denver papers to devote extensive coverage to Columbine over the past two years. In the paper's

November 5, 2000, issue, Pulitzer Prize–winning reporter Dave Curtin wrote an article that clearly demonstrated how much emotional resonance Columbine held for young people preparing to enter college.

For his article, Curtin talked to college admission deans across the nation who said the Columbine horror was the most popular admissions essay topic in the last two years.

Curtin said that before Columbine, students wrote about simpler topics: their favorite teacher, an influential relative, or a memorable moment from a winning ball game. But now student essays are exploring deeper issues.

"It really grounded them to say, 'What am I going to do with the rest of my life?'" observed one admissions counselor, who said 240 applicants—or about half the incoming freshmen—wrote about Columbine. "It was quick maturity for a lot of them. I can't say there's been an event where we even had one-half the interest that this generated."

"I think it says that Columbine was an event which made a huge impact on these students," one admissions director said. "It makes me wonder whether Columbine is this generation's Kent State. It's really a defining moment in their teen lives."

Another admissions official said: "I think kids are starting to realize the danger that the world holds. They are coming to the conclusion that they are vulnerable creatures."

One school even allowed Curtin to take a look at some of the students' essays. Read what some of them had to say:

There is no sense of unity, and we are divided into the infamous cliques that have only recently made the news, in connection with the massacre in Littleton, Colorado. When one constantly physically and emotionally knocks down those who could be potential allies, any idea of unity is destroyed. Without unity, the voices are separated and too weak to be heard.

The schools where violence occurs do not suspect it, and many times students are injured or killed. It's happening everywhere. How are students supposed to feel safe when it could be their school next? The shooting at Columbine High School made many people aware of the reality of school violence. Yet, the violence has not ceased.

Right after the Columbine incident there was a hit list on the Internet for my high school. This scared me so much that I did not want to go to school. One day there were rumors flying around school of a bombing at noon. I left school that day along with many other students. Being scared and running away is not the way to go through school.

A possible solution to school violence would be making a mandatory class for students to discuss their views on school violence. They would share ideas on stopping school violence and preventing violence in their school.

Last year after the dreadful Columbine shooting, ninth graders in my school did not come to school for a week because they were so petrified of being shot or attacked. Students should not have to go to school every day wondering if that day is going to be the day.

Because of fear in the community, our school has canceled many school-related activities. Pep rallies that boost school spirit were canceled because it was an open risk for any kind of violence.

Once in a while, an issue comes along that hits home to every person in this country. One such case was the school shootings that occurred in Colorado. The truly horrible thing is that it could happen anywhere.

At Columbine High School shots were fired that were heard around the nation. [It] affected every parent, student, and teacher. This has gone down in history as the worst U.S. tragedy. The shootings alerted the nation that there are problems in our society that must be faced and rules must be changed.

When choosing a college my main concern is the safety and security that the college can give to its students. The Columbine shooting caused everyone to be scared and nervous.

Two Years—From Terror to Tranquillity

For me, April 20, 1999, was a day that began much like many other days but quickly turned into a day that I will never, ever forget.

My cell phone rang around noon. It was my fiancée, Sandy, asking if I had heard the news. "There's been a shooting at Columbine," she said.

I dropped what I was doing, jumped into my truck, and rushed across town, listening to a local radio station as I went. The station was broadcasting sketchy accounts of multiple shootings. As I drove, I could feel my heart pounding nearly out of my chest. I was terrified and feeling increasingly agitated. I felt close to hyperventilating and hoped that I wouldn't have a heart attack right there in my truck.

As I crept along in the bumper-to-bumper traffic, I had a real concern for Rachel. It would be many hours later that I finally learned that she had been killed.

I wrote in my earlier book, *Rachel's Tears: The Spiritual Journey of Columbine Martyr Rachel Scott* (Thomas Nelson, 2000), that as I drove toward the school that day, I had a vivid impression that this unfolding tragedy was a spiritual event. I had no idea what that meant at the time, but over the next two years it would become much clearer to me. There were numerous magazines such as *Time* and *Newsweek* that chronicled the spiritual awakening among the youth of America in the days that followed Columbine's tragedy. I personally saw this awakening firsthand as I spoke to over a million people during the next two years.

Littleton, Colorado, was so flooded with stories about Columbine through television and newspapers that eventually the community experienced a degree of "burnout." Josh McDowell, Governor Owens, and Michael W. Smith helped me host a memorial service on the first anniversary of the tragedy. The media once again brought their focus back to Columbine, and they were surprised that so few showed up at the school or the park nearby. It was estimated that over half a million people would be there, when in fact only a few thousand showed up.

Outside the Littleton area, however, I have found that people were not burned out over Columbine. Many of them wanted to know as much as they could about the lives of Rachel and the other victims. Just as my generation will always have a vulnerable place in our hearts concerning John F. Kennedy's death, Rachel's generation will always have sad and vivid memories of April 20, 1999, and the deaths of their peers and one brave teacher.

Picking Up the Torch

The message Rachel left behind by her acts of kindness and her writings compelled all the members of our family to proclaim her story to the world.

My eldest daughter, Bethanee McCandless, gave of herself in answering thousands of phone calls and E-mails from around the world that poured in as a result of Rachel's life and death. My second eldest daughter, Dana, began speaking in schools, churches, and community centers around the nation. Craig and Mike, my two sons, have traveled to different events with my wife, Sandy, and me.

Sandy, Rachel's stepmom, gave up her job as a beautician to travel with me and help with presentations. Together we have spoken to over one million people, not including those reached through the countless TV, radio, and newspaper interviews.

Rachel and the Columbine tragedy inspired to action the leaders of numerous Christian organizations:

- Josh McDowell did a series of "911" events and shared Rachel's story with millions of people worldwide. Josh featured me on a radio broadcast that brought a huge outpouring of response, and he also helped us host the first anniversary memorial service in Littleton.

- Ron Luce, the head of Teen Mania, challenged hundreds of thousands of young people to do missions work in Rachel's memory. I personally talked to dozens who told me they spent their summer in some foreign missions field on Rachel's behalf.

- Bruce Porter, the pastor of a Littleton church who founded TorchGrab Ministries, not only conducted mass rallies around the country but also wrote a book based on Rachel's testimony entitled *The Martyr's Torch*.

- Bob Weiner, founder of Maranatha Ministries, took one year away from his normal work and speaking to specifically challenge young people with Rachel's story.

We continue to be amazed at the massive positive impact generated by the simple acts of kindness Rachel performed. (Our nonprofit organization, The Columbine Redemption, seeks to perpetuate her good works by providing a source of information and healing to all those affected by the tragedy. For information, visit our Web site at www.thecolumbineredemption.com.)

Postelection Pandemonium

On November 8, 2000, the eyes of much of the nation were on Palm Beach, Florida, where controversy was already breaking out over the uncertain results of the previous day's presidential election. Dana, Sandy, and I were in Palm Beach that night to speak about Rachel and Columbine.

I thought that because of the hullabaloo about the election there would be a small crowd to hear us, but the four-thousand-seat auditorium was packed to capacity. Another thousand or so people who hadn't been able to make it in crowded outside the building.

I was a little amazed that at a time of growing national confusion over the election so many people would come out to hear us talk about an event that had occurred a year and a half before.

It's obvious why young people come to such events. Many of the adults have told me their kids brought them.

Sometimes after I speak, young people just drape themselves over me and sob their hearts out. Some of them have been picked on by others and have decided they're going to make a difference in their schools. In other cases, kids who have picked on others talk to me. I've had school bullies come up to me with tears streaming down their faces to say, "Mr. Scott, I've been guilty of picking on kids, but after hearing Rachel's story, I'm making a commitment to pick up her torch and make a difference in my school."

Back at the office of The Columbine Redemption, Bethanee has collected ten volumes containing thousands of hard copies of E-mail sent to us by young people at the high schools, colleges, football stadiums, civic auditoriums, churches, or outdoor fields in the towns and cities where we've spoken.

The feedback has just been incredible, and it confirms my belief that this generation of young people is looking for role models. Many young people have been disappointed by the athletes or politicians they might otherwise look up to as role models; they're now looking to their own generation. Rachel is just one of a number of role models who have been brought to the public eye as a result of Columbine and who speak to young people's hunger for authenticity and passion. The kids tell me they want to know more of her story.

A Tale of Two Books

Rachel's Tears came out on the first anniversary of the Columbine tragedy and was mostly a spiritual biography of Rachel. That book, which her mother and I wrote, talked about our reactions to Rachel's death as well as Rachel's deep spiritual values, which were based on her unshakable faith in God.

Chain Reaction is a different kind of book. Instead of focusing on Rachel, this book deals with her ideas on topics like compassion, kindness, love, and forgiveness, and how to apply them in our lives.

Rachel knew that the world could be a violent place, but she believed that the only effective antidote to violence was acts of kindness. In this book we'll be looking more at the things Rachel did rather than who she was, although you can't really separate the two.

Rachel firmly believed that if she did something for someone else, it was going to be multiplied many times. Possibly, this blessing intended for others would come back around like a boomerang and result in a blessing to her as well.

Among the people Rachel reached out to were Eric Harris and Dylan Klebold, the two troubled young men who unleashed the tragedy that Columbine is now known for. Some people have even suggested to me that it was her outreach to Eric and Dylan that killed her. I don't know.

But the truth of the matter is, everything Rachel did has now been amplified by her death. She had written that she would be willing to pay any price to live according to her personal code and to see her actions multiplied. Now, the chain reaction she wrote and dreamed and prayed about has begun to reach around the world.

Kindness Can Be Tough

One of the things we'll be talking about a lot in this book is compassionate acts of kindness. But we need to clarify right away that to Rachel, kindness was not some kind of namby-pamby, nicey-nice, goody-two-shoes approach. She could be very direct with people like Eric and Dylan, whom she criticized for creating videos for class assignments that were full of violence and curses.

For Rachel, compassion and kindness could be acts of bravery. She was someone who went against the grain. Often, she knew it was going to cost her something to live according to her values. If she reached out to kids who were low on the school totem pole, people who were interested in social position stayed away from her. And when she confronted bullies, some kids stayed away from her because they wanted to avoid trouble at any cost.

But it was exactly this kind of selfless sacrifice that makes her story so powerful, and that enables her to continue to have an impact on young people around the world. I can see some of this impact when I speak about Rachel and her actions. Now, in this book, I can share some of her ideas with people I will never be able to meet personally.

Whether you read my words in this book or hear them at a large gathering, the message is the same. Rachel's life is a call to revolution. It's a revolution of kindness. It's a revolution of compassion.

Triumph Amidst Tragedy

Speaker and writer Zig Ziglar had a big impact on my life in my early years, and he said something that has stuck with me for a long, long time.

His words have now become a cliché, but they are still true. Ziglar said that when life hands you a lemon, you should turn it into lemonade.

Believe me when I say that there's no bigger lemon than to lose your beloved child. In the months and years after Columbine, I have applauded many of the Columbine parents who have done what they believed was the right thing to honor their children. Some have become active in the fight for gun control even though they were never involved in politics before their children died.

Some have fought long and hard for a change in police and SWAT team tactics so that future school shootings may result in fewer lives being lost. Their efforts have already borne some fruit.

Although I'm taking a different approach, I'm doing what I need to do to honor Rachel. It would be impossible for me to simply mourn her loss and ignore the legacy she left through her writings and her life. To do this would be a tragedy on top of a tragedy.

Instead, I speak and I write about her message. I do so because I believe that this tragedy can ultimately be turned into a triumph. I believe her life can be the spark plug for literally thousands— maybe millions—of young people who are moved by her words and her example. And while it's difficult for me to say so, I believe that this was a part of her purpose from the time she was born— to have an impact on other people through her life and through her death.

Reports from Ground Zero

The day after the Columbine killings, Jonathan and Stephen Cohen, two brothers who attended the school, wrote a song about the tragedy called "Friend of Mine." They sang the song at the April 25 Columbine memorial service, which was attended by an estimated seventy thousand people and was broadcast live by CNN to a worldwide viewing audience.

In the song, the Cohen brothers affirm their belief that hope can emerge from horror:

> Columbine, rose blood red, heartbreak overflows my head.
> Columbine, friend of mine.
> Peace will come to you in time.
> Columbine, friend of mine.

I hope you hear the message of hope in their song and this book. It's a message that helps us move from mourning over the past to creating a new future for us all.

2
Lessons from a Tragedy

By April 21, 1999, one day after the tragedy at Columbine, reporters for newspapers and television networks from around the country were already telling the world that Columbine was the most deadly episode of school violence in the nation's history.

But over the next year, as more details about the killing spree emerged, it became clear that many, many more students could have been killed. As one Littleton Fire Department official put it, "It could have been so much worse."

I don't enjoy reviewing the grisly events of this tragedy, but I do so to illustrate two tremendously important truths. First, we all have choices that we must make in life. And second, the kinds of choices we consistently make throughout our lives reveal much about our deepest-held feelings and beliefs.

Design for Destruction

Denver Post reporter Peggy Lowe wrote:

When Eric Harris and Dylan Klebold launched their attack on Columbine High School they carried 95 explosive devices in all—enough firepower to wipe out their school and potentially hundreds of students.

Forty-eight carbon dioxide bombs, or "crickets." Twenty-seven pipe bombs. Eleven 1.5-gallon propane containers. Seven incendiary devices with 40-plus gallons of flammable liquid. Two duffel bag bombs with 20-pound liquefied-petroleum gas tanks. (Feb. 14, 2000)

The attack was much more than a mere spur-of-the-moment outburst. The killers had spent months planning their attack and building their many devices, many of which thankfully failed to explode.

The *Denver Post* article summarizes the Columbine killers' deadly arsenal. Pipe bombs were placed at a nearby intersection to divert law enforcement people away from the school. Additional bombs were placed outside the school, inside the school, in the killers' parents' homes, and in the two killers' cars.

One of the bombs, which they placed near a doorway to the school, was filled with gas and had nails and buckshot attached with duct tape. Another bomb, which was strategically located near the doorway to the school's crowded library, was attached to a quart of homemade napalm.

Harris and Klebold had placed a pair of propane bombs in the school's cafeteria. They were attached to a timer set to detonate the bombs during a crowded lunch period. Had they gone off, the bombs could have killed hundreds of students. The killers also planned to set up their guns outside the cafeteria so they could systematically mow down surviving students fleeing from the cafeteria.

The car bombs—one in the back seat of Harris's Honda and the other in Klebold's BMW—were designed to wreak havoc and death in the school's parking lot. Both were wired to timers set for noon. Investigators suggested that the timing was designed to injure or kill investigators who might be exploring the two cars.

One bomb expert who investigated the scene declared that this was more than a simple school-shooting scenario. "I look at Columbine High School as a true act of domestic terrorism," said the investigator.

Another investigator summarized things this way: "Thank God these people weren't good bomb-makers."

Months after the *Post* article was published, results of an official investigation conducted by the Jefferson County Sheriff's Department were released. This report—which was so voluminous that it was released only on CD-ROM—contained equally chilling details.

According to *USA Today*, the contents of the report included a detailed, minute-by-minute accounting of the deadly forty-nine-minute assault, crime scene photographs, some of the killers' writings, maps of their route through the school, audio clips of 911 emergency calls and police radio traffic, and previously unreleased surveillance videotape from the school cafeteria showing the killers shooting guns and throwing bombs, apparently in an attempt to detonate larger bombs that had failed to explode.

Throughout the last two years, investigators have examined more than 10,000 pieces of evidence, conducted 4,500 interviews, and performed 3,500 ballistic examinations. Although their reports were thorough and detailed, they failed to answer the one question that was the most important: Why?

A Parent's Aftermath

I was not aware of any of these details in the days after the Columbine killings. Even if I had been aware of them, I'm not sure I would have understood them very well. When you first lose a child or a loved one, you're not thinking about any of these things. You're thinking only about your grief.

All I could think about is that I was not going to see Rachel again. I would never see her smile again. I would never again sit down with her and have one of our wonderful talks.

It was at least a month after her death that I first began to think about the enormity of the tragedy. Slowly, I began analyzing some of the information that had been out there. It took me a while to comprehend what I was seeing, but as I began to consciously recognize the sheer audacity of the attack, I began to feel angry.

The more I thought about the whole tragedy, what really hit me was the fact that these boys had spent so much time planning this whole attack. This wasn't merely a simple and sudden act of revenge on one student or teacher. This was a deliberate, well-designed plan for a mass murder.

As the truth began to sink in, all I could ask was, Why? Why did they take the time to make so many bombs? Why did they take the time to do all the things they did?

The more I asked these questions, the more I was forced to look beyond the data provided in police reports and ballistics tests. I knew I must try to look into the souls of the two killers. I had the opportunity to do that shortly before Christmas, 1999.

Videos of Hate

I was in Dallas, Texas, preparing to speak at Josh McDowell's annual Christmas banquet for his employees when the news broke that *Time* magazine was revealing the contents of the videos Eric and Dylan had made.

The cover featured an image from a Columbine surveillance camera showing Eric Harris and Dylan Klebold in action. The twenty-page cover story included comments the killers had made in a series of videotapes they recorded during the months before the killings.

Like many of the other victims' families, I was shocked by the content of these videos. We were all upset at Sheriff Stone for allowing the world to know the contents of those tapes without letting us, at the very least, see them first. He should have at least warned us that the media would be publishing them. I called a press conference and was joined by a number of the victims' families in asking for the sheriff's resignation.

But what stunned me the most was the fact that Eric and Dylan talked about Rachel on their videos, making fun of her faith. They referred to her as a "godly Christian" and then threw in some vulgarity.

They obviously shared an intense hostility toward Christianity. "What would Jesus do?" asked Klebold, yelling and making faces at the camera while referring to a WWJD wristband that Rachel wore. He then yelled, "What would I do?" and pointed an imaginary gun at the camera, took aim, and said, "Boosh!"

"Yeah, I love Jesus. I love Jesus. Shut the [expletive] up," Harris said on the same tape, which was made a little over a month before the killings.

I was very disturbed as I watched those videos, not only by what they said about Rachel, but also with their intense hatred toward anything Christian.

Immediately upon viewing the videos, I realized that a combination of simmering rage, resentment for fellow students, and a desire for celebrity spurred Eric Harris and Dylan Klebold to gun down their fellow students. As I watched, I began to understand a little more about the souls of the two young men who had not only gone after Christian students but who also seemed to have targeted blacks and jocks for death.

An Inner Vacuum

In time, more and more material about these two troubled young men began to surface. The more I read, the more clearly I began to see that there was a yawning spiritual vacuum deep inside them that they were desperately trying to fill up any way they could.

USA Today published a chilling article that included insights from the killers' journals and other documents:

> The day before he and Eric Harris launched their assault on Columbine High School, Dylan Klebold wrote in his notebook a detailed itinerary for the attack. "When first bombs go off, attack." It concluded: "Have fun!"
>
> Harris also wrote an itinerary in his day planner. His last entry: "HAHAHA."
>
> But it wasn't all fun and games for these killers. Elsewhere Eric Harris had written these sad words: "I am full of hate, and I love it."

I found all of these words both troubling and revealing as I sought to understand the souls of the two young men who killed my daughter and others at Columbine. But the words I found to be the most troubling came from the video Eric and Dylan recorded on March 15, 1999.

Looking at the camera, Harris said, "We need a [expletive] kick start—we need to get a chain reaction going here!"

Eric's words stunned me because Rachel had also talked of

starting a chain reaction of her own using acts of kindness. As she said in the paper she wrote for a class at school, "I have this theory that if one person can go out of their way to show compassion, then it will start a chain reaction of the same. People will never know how far a little kindness can go."

The amazing thing to me was that these statements were made at the same time, in March of 1999, just one month before the tragedy. It was as though these two teenagers laid down a double challenge to their entire generation.

As I thought about the two statements—Eric Harris's hate-filled declaration of his intent to start a chain reaction of violence and Rachel's pledge to launch a chain reaction of kindness—I was troubled.

Rachel was responding to the love she felt for people and trying to start a chain reaction that spread that love to others.

On the other hand, Eric Harris, a person I believe was a sensitive soul and a deep thinker, had gone to the core of his being and found nothing. Out of the feelings of nothingness and hatred he had bottled up inside, he dreamed of launching a chain reaction of violence and death.

There's no way to harmonize these two views, so I tried to express my feelings about them by writing the following song. The first verse talks about Eric's plan, while the second verse explores Rachel's plan, and the third verse is about my own plan, which emerged in the months after the tragedy.

Chain Reaction

by Darrell Scott [copyright 2000]

Two angry boys, charting a plan
Guided by forces they don't understand

One of them yells, "I'll make them pay!
I won't let anyone get in my way!"

I'm gonna start a chain reaction
I will not stop till I have satisfaction
I am consumed by agitation
I'll make a difference in my generation
       I'll be a part, with all of my heart
       I'm gonna start—a chain reaction

Pretty young girl, writing it down
Walking her talk, 'cause she knows she has found
Light for her life, watch her now shine
Mercy in action and words that are kind

I'm gonna start a chain reaction
I will not stop till I have satisfaction
I am consumed by inspiration
I'll make a difference in my generation
       I'll be a part, with all of my heart
       I'm gonna start—a chain reaction

They are now gone, I'm here today
Facing the choices that God brings my way
Life can be hard, and I understand
But I'm committed to do what I can

I'm gonna start a chain reaction
I will not stop till I have satisfaction
I am consumed by inspiration
I'll make a difference in my generation

I'll be a part, with all of my heart
I'm gonna start—a chain reaction

The rest of this book is designed to challenge you to think about your life and the kind of chain reactions you can create. The choice is yours. You can try to set in motion a positive revolution or a negative one, a life-giving revolution or a life-destroying one.

Either way, you have been given tremendous gifts and responsibilities. I hope you use them in the best way.

A Broader Moral Vacuum

I mentioned Eric Harris and how he looked deep within his own soul and saw nothing there. The causes of this emptiness are varied and complex. It is something none of us will be able to understand totally.

In the months after Columbine I have been troubled to learn about the moral vacuum that exists in many schools around our country. Too often, it seems, lost souls like Eric Harris do not receive the guidance they need because administrators or teachers mistakenly feel they are legally prohibited from teaching students about the differences between good and evil, between moral deeds and immoral deeds.

If there is one positive thing that has come out of the whole Columbine tragedy, it is that the severity of the violence and the planning the killers put into it have served as a shocking wake-up call to the need to put a greater emphasis on pointing out the differences between right and wrong, light and dark.

Law enforcement personnel learned similar lessons from

Columbine. Prior to Columbine, officers dealing with a school-shooting situation would wait for backup from other officers and would then secure the school. But following Columbine, there were charges that some of the people who died would have lived if police had responded more quickly and more aggressively.

According to a recent story in the *Denver Post*, "The tragedy of the Columbine High massacre has forever changed the way police will respond to school shootings." Now, said the article, police will try to enter a school as quickly as possible instead of waiting for SWAT teams and other backup to arrive.

I hope that the rest of us can learn other lessons from Columbine. The lesson I hope we learn is that there are big and important differences between good and evil, and between love and hate, and we better start figuring out which side we are on and which values we are going to promote with our lives.

Reading, Writing, and Right and Wrong

I remember hearing a speaker once who said something that perfectly captures the moral vacuum I'm talking about. The man simply said this:

> Today, it's possible to go to a school where you can get a degree in making weapons and war. Or you can go to another school where you can get a degree in medicine and nursing. But it's difficult to find a school which will tell you which type of degree is better for the human race.

I think that is often the case. There is a big vacuum when it comes to spelling out the differences between right and wrong.

But as simple experiments in science class can show, nature abhors a vacuum. Similarly, in terms of our human nature, where there is a vacuum, something will be pulled in to fill it.

The problems our schools face today have a lot to do with social changes that began taking place in the 1960s. In the earlier chapter, I suggested that the assassination of John F. Kennedy was a defining moment for many people in my generation. Unfortunately, this tragedy was only one of many things creating tremendous uncertainty in that turbulent decade.

Today, it is hard for us to recall how different things were back then. Blacks, who were struggling for basic equality in society, founded the Civil Rights movement, which exposed racism. Women, who often did the same work as men but were paid much less, began the women's movement, which aimed to give women some of the same freedoms men had. At the same time there was a tremendous influx of Eastern religious movements as well as the creation of many new spiritual groups and practices.

All of this left many people feeling very destabilized. As long-established roles between the races and the sexes were overturned, people didn't know exactly what to do or how to behave. For example, was opening a door for a woman a good thing to do that she would appreciate, or would it be perceived as demeaning and sexist?

Along the way, many people gave up on saying anything was right or anything else was wrong. Tolerance and a respect for people's natural differences turned into a total inability to make important moral distinctions. A lot of this moral confusion got passed along to our nation's schools.

In the wake of Columbine, political leaders were willing to consider any means to make schools safer for our kids. Some said schools needed more security guards and x-ray machines. Others said the problem was lack of strong gun control laws. My personal challenge to our leaders was to look at the possibility that we are facing a moral and spiritual crisis because of the vacuum that was created when we removed every shred of spiritual influence from our schools in the '60s.

In May 1999, I was asked to go before a House Judiciary Committee and speak to our nation's leaders in the same room where the Nixon and Clinton impeachment hearings took place. The following is part of that speech:

I wrote a poem four nights ago, before I knew I would be speaking here today, that expresses my feelings best.

Your laws ignore our deepest needs
Your words are empty air
You've stripped away our heritage
You've outlawed simple prayer

Now gunshots fill our classrooms
And precious children die
You seek for answers everywhere
And ask the question "Why?"

A Different Time

It may be hard for some of today's students to understand how much things have changed in American history, but a quick look at a series of books called the McGuffey Readers will illustrate where we have come from and where we are going.

During the late 1800s and early 1900s, the McGuffey Readers

were required reading for students in many of America's schools. One of the main goals of this popular series was to teach children moral lessons. The purpose wasn't just to teach young people reading, writing, and arithmetic, but to present moral lessons along with their other learning.

The McGuffey Readers were full of chapters with titles like these:

"Why Is It Important to Be Kind?"
"The Power of Forgiveness"
"Consequences of Idleness"
"Advantages of Industry"
"Perseverance"
"Try, Try Again"
"The Good Son"
"Waste Not, Want Not"
"The Right Way"
"The Golden Rule"
"The Way to Be Happy"
"Dare to Do Right"

The writing wasn't preachy or judgmental, but these books did insist that there was an important moral difference between hate and love, or between helping someone out and hurting him.

I'm afraid we've lost much of that in our contemporary educational system, and I believe I see the consequences of that loss in our schools' declining SAT scores, in our growing rates of juvenile crime, in the rapid increase of teen pregnancies and sexually transmitted diseases, and in a number of other problems.

We have become so afraid to label anything right or wrong that moral issues are rarely even dealt with. As a result, we now have an educational system that is politically correct and morally neutral. But ultimately, neutrality is a void. It's a vacuum. Something is going to fill it. For lost and lonely kids like Eric Harris and Dylan Klebold, hate filled the vacuum.

One of the reasons I am writing this book is to help students who are offered such a morally empty education to find their own creative means to live out the kind of positive moral values on which Rachel based her life. This book may not provide the cure for all of society's ills or all of the problems schools face today, but treatment of many symptoms such as intimidation and violence in schools can begin with people practicing acts of compassion and kindness.

Wouldn't you prefer that people treated you with love rather than hate? As you think back over important moments in your life, haven't some of the most meaningful instances been those times when people went out of their way to help you?

As we will see in the next chapter, kindness sometimes sounds as if it's something gooey and sweet, but throughout history, great men and women like Abraham Lincoln, Martin Luther King Jr., Mother Teresa, and Gandhi have been men and women of kindness.

A Common Calling

Maybe you don't feel like you're a Mother Teresa or a Gandhi. Maybe instead of being a spiritual superstar you're just an ordinary person. That's OK. Rachel and Eric Harris were ordinary kids too.

Sometimes I have the tendency to make Rachel sound as if she was some kind of saint whose feet never touched the ground. But that is not the case. Just ask her brothers and sisters. Rachel was a good girl, but she had her problems. The important thing she proved with her life is the difference one person can make when she decides to start a chain reaction of compassion and kindness.

Eric Harris wasn't all evil either. I may make it sound that way, but if things had turned out differently and Eric had not killed the students at Columbine and himself, I believe that it would be easy for us to find things about him that were good or that we liked.

Rachel and Eric made some significant choices about what they were going to do with their lives, and those choices led to a series of consequences.

The question now is what you are going to do with your life and the decisions that face you. What values are you going to live by? What impact are you going to make in the world? What kind of chain reaction are you going to start?

I think every person can have a burning sense of destiny in life, and part of the purpose of this book is to ignite that flame. My hope and prayer are that you will develop confidence in your unique skills and gifts and find ways you can creatively use these gifts to spread compassion and kindness among the people you know.

Before Columbine, Rachel was a high school kid trying to live out her beliefs. She had a strong sense of destiny, and she was look-ing to the future. She also had strong premonitions about the vio-lence that would disrupt her school.

On the other hand, I don't believe she knew what kind of impact her life would have after her death. She had no way of knowing that a diary she wrote only for herself would be seen by millions of people, that the president of the United States would have it in his hands, or that Elton John would be moved by it.

She didn't know any of these things. She simply took one step at a time. It was faithfulness in the many little steps of life that helped her start a chain reaction. By focusing on faithfulness in the little things in your life, you can do the same.

3
The Ripple Effect

The cover of this book features a photo that illustrates what I feel is one of the most important lessons we can learn in life. Next to Rachel's face is an image of the surface of a pond. The camera, which has permanently frozen a split second of action for us to see, gives us a glimpse of something amazing in progress.

We can see the ripples spreading over the surface of the water. If the photographer continued shooting additional pictures, we might be able to see the ripples spreading ever outward until they cover the entire surface of the pond. But we only see this one instant, so we will never know how far the ripples will go.

At the center of the ripples a column of water appears to be standing straight up. This is a spontaneous reaction of the water to whatever was dropped into the pond. This shows us that the reaction is strongest at the point of impact. Nevertheless, the effect spreads throughout the pond.

There is another important thing this photo reveals to us—or doesn't reveal to us. We only see the surface of the water, so we cannot tell what was dropped into the pond. Perhaps it was a tiny pebble. We will never know, because whatever it was, it is now invisible. All that remain are the ripples spreading across the pond's surface.

I think this is a truly amazing photograph. It shows us so many things that would have escaped our attention if the camera hadn't made everything stop so we could see what was happening at that particular moment in time.

The lessons we can draw from this photo are equally important. For example, there is no such thing as a little action. No matter who you are or what you do, in some way you start a ripple effect similar to the stone dropping in the water.

This is true no matter how large the stone or seemingly significant the action. Our culture is fascinated with celebrities, whether they are performers, athletes, business leaders, or politicians. We can think of these celebrities as the big boulders of our world. But the truth is that it's the little pebbles that start most of the ripples that impact our daily lives.

History is full of examples of little-known people who did seemingly simple things that had a profound effect on people around them. The movie *Forrest Gump* deals with this truth in a humorous way. As a means of dealing with the big and little struggles in his life, Forrest decided to start running. A large group of people soon began following him back and forth across the continent, trying to understand Forrest's philosophical reasons for running. Major networks began reporting his actions, and publications featured him on their covers.

The question I want to ask you is a simple one, but one that is extremely important. What kind of ripple effect will you be causing as you live your life? What chain reactions will result from your thoughts, words, and actions?

As we discussed in the previous chapter, my daughter, Rachel Scott, and the gunman who killed her, Eric Harris, wanted to start a chain reaction. Both did, and today the ripples from their actions continue to impact people in both big and little ways.

Eric Harris's actions at Columbine impacted your life immediately. Remember how you felt when you first heard of the shootings. Remember your thoughts, your fears, and perhaps your tears, as you watched the tragedy as it played out before your eyes on television. Today you are feeling the ripple effect from Rachel's life as you read this book.

Perhaps you have never thought of yourself as someone who would have any real impact on the world. Maybe you concluded long ago that you are too small to cause any ripples, and that only big boulders can make a significant splash in life. That kind of thinking not only prevents you from realizing the powerful potential you have but also diminishes the impact you may be having on others.

One of the ways we are going to explore these issues is by taking a look at the lives of some people who have created chain reaction ripples of compassion. Years ago, John F. Kennedy wrote a book called *Profiles in Courage*. Perhaps we could call the mini-biographies in the following pages "Profiles in Compassion."

I hope you find these stories encouraging. More important, I hope you see in these lives examples of the ways people have changed the world by practicing compassion in both little and big ways.

Loving the Least of the Least

You probably do not recognize the name Agnes Gonxha Bojaxhiu. But I believe that this woman, who died in 1997, was one of the most compassionate people to live in the twentieth century. Perhaps you know her better by her more popular name: Mother Teresa.

She was born on August 27, 1910, in Shkup, which was then part of the Ottoman Empire. She grew up very comfortably, for her family was very wealthy, but when she turned eighteen, she decided to turn her back on all that her family had to offer her. Instead, she went far away to Ireland where she entered the Sisters of Loreto convent as a novice.

As a result of this decision, her family members turned their backs on her and declared that she would never inherit the vast sums of money they had earlier promised her.

A year later, this tiny young woman was sent to India, an over-crowded and poverty-stricken country. By 1931 she was teaching at a Calcutta girls' school. She did this work faithfully for the next fifteen years. Though she was not yet famous, she was starting a chain reac-tion among India's young women. The ripples of her work were spreading out among the hundreds and hundreds of girls she taught.

Then in 1946, a funny thing happened. Agnes Gonxha Bojaxhiu said she heard God calling her to live and work among the poor. I don't know about you, but if I was planning to be somebody important in life, I don't think this is the direction I would go. It would be much easier to be famous by hanging around with rich celebrities, not poor people who died on the streets because they didn't have enough money to buy food or basic medical care.

She remained faithful to her vision, creating a new order of nuns called the Missionaries of Charity, which was officially sanc-tioned by the pope in 1950. Long before she was a world renowned celebrity, Mother Teresa was a humble woman who spent nearly fifty years faithfully living out her vision, caring for terminally ill and destitute people who came to the Kalighat

Temple—a Hindu shrine—to die. Mother Teresa and her fellow sisters—who wore Indian saris instead of the Western clothing favored by other Catholic orders—embraced these people, took them to their center, and lovingly cared for them during their final days and hours. Many people looked the other way, refusing to see Calcutta's dying people. But Mother Teresa wanted them to die surrounded by dignity and love.

The rest is history. In 1963, this frail woman now known as Mother Teresa was awarded India's Padmashri Award for services to the people of India. In 1979 she won the Nobel Peace Prize. On September 5, 1997, she died in her beloved Calcutta. Her funeral was broadcast on TV around the world. Many people believe she will soon be named a saint.

Standing Against the Tide

Mother Teresa exemplified the love of one willing to reach out to the untouchables of society. Here in America centuries of racism created a similar group of outcasts. The following profile in compassion focuses on a man who, though himself a member of the downtrodden group, had the vision, courage, and compassion to stand tall and lead the way to peace and justice.

African-Americans were first enslaved and forced to work on white people's farms and plantations. The Civil War was supposed to end all this, but a century later blacks were still struggling to enjoy simple freedoms such as voting in elections, working at the same kinds of jobs whites had, or even freely walking in some parts of major towns. Throughout the South, racist bullies used terror and intimidation to keep blacks "in their place." When these tactics didn't work, they lynched blacks for getting "uppity."

Time magazine writer Jack E. White further described the conditions African-Americans were enduring when Martin Luther King Jr. began making ripples in his pond:

> A six-year-old black girl like Ruby Bridges could be hectored and spit on by a white New Orleans mob simply because she wanted to go to the same school as white children. A fourteen-year-old black boy like Emmett Till could be hunted down and murdered by a Mississippi gang simply because he had supposedly made suggestive remarks to a white woman. Even highly educated blacks were routinely denied the right to vote or serve on juries. They could not eat at lunch counters, register in motels or use whites-only rest rooms; they could not buy or rent a home wherever they chose. In some rural enclaves in the South, they were even compelled to get off the sidewalk and stand in the street if a Caucasian walked by.

It was against this backdrop that Martin Luther King Jr. decided to make his stand for freedom and justice.

In 1954, the same year the U.S. Supreme Court declared segregation in public schools unconstitutional, King was called to pastor the Dexter Avenue Baptist Church in Montgomery, Alabama. The following year, Rosa Parks ignited the Montgomery bus boycott, generally regarded as the first major campaign of the modern Civil Rights movement, and King became its leader.

The August 1963 March on Washington brought more than 250,000 people to the nation's capital where they heard King's rousing "I Have A Dream" speech, which is probably one of the most famous speeches in American history:

> I say to you today, my friends, that in spite of the difficulties and frustrations of the moment, I still have a dream. It is a dream

deeply rooted in the American dream.

I have a dream that one day this nation will rise up and live out the true meaning of its creed: "We hold these truths to be self-evident: that all men are created equal."

I have a dream that one day on the red hills of Georgia the sons of former slaves and the sons of former slave owners will be able to sit down together at a table of brotherhood.

I have a dream that one day even the state of Mississippi, a desert state, sweltering with the heat of injustice and oppression, will be transformed into an oasis of freedom and justice.

White also described King's personal encounters with bullies:

A threatening telephone call at midnight alarmed him: "Nigger, we are tired of you and your mess now. And if you aren't out of this town in three days, we're going to blow your brains out and blow up your house." Shaken, King went to the kitchen to pray. "I could hear an inner voice saying to me, 'Martin Luther, stand up for righteousness. Stand up for justice. Stand up for truth. And I will be with you, even until the end of the world.'"

King followed his dream no matter what the cost, and for his courage he was awarded the Nobel Peace Prize in 1964. He continued to fight for civil rights until April 1968. He was assassinated one day after telling a Memphis audience, "I've seen the promised land. I may not get there with you, but I want you to know tonight that we as a people will get to the promised land."

King's deep faith and his unshakable commitment enabled him to stand against the tide. Today, nearly every major city in the U.S. has a street or school named after King. The ripples from his actions continue to spread around the world. I was privileged to meet and speak on the same platform with Bernice King, Dr. Martin Luther King's daughter. His son Martin Luther King III attended our memorial service at the one-year anniversary of Columbine's tragedy and he graciously assented to my request that he share a few words with the audience.

Saints or Bullies?

In the months after the Columbine killings, everyone tried to understand what had happened and why. Parents wanted to understand why their children had been injured or killed. Teachers and school administrators wanted to learn how a school had become a killing ground. The entire Littleton community and much of the world wanted to know how two troubled teens could cause so much harm.

Colorado Governor Bill Owens established the Columbine Review Commission to hear testimony about the attacks. One of the facts that emerged from the commission's October 2000 hearings was that bullying was a significant problem at Columbine High.

Although some denied that bullying was a problem, special education teacher Patti Stevens disagreed, testifying through her tears about the abuse her students had routinely endured.

According to a report about the hearing published in the *Denver Post*, Stevens, who was in the cafeteria with her special education students on the day of the murders, described rampant bullying at Columbine in the two years before the April 20, 1999, attack. She said one of the school's "jocks" singled out her kids for especially cruel treatment.

"I saw how afraid and scared my special education kids were," she said. "I mentioned it at staff meetings. I didn't get any response. They kind of blew me off."

Stevens also said members of a group called the Trench Coat Mafia, which included Eric Harris and Dylan Klebold among its unofficial members, often hung out at the Southwest Plaza Mall, about a mile west of the school. She and other witnesses testified that the group members bullied people inside the shopping center.

Betty Shoels, the aunt of student Isaiah Shoels, said the Trench Coat Mafia harassed Isaiah daily. Isaiah was killed while trying to hide under a school library table with my son Craig. Isaiah's aunt said, "They'd go down the halls harassing kids, making racial slurs, and not just racial slurs, harassing people they didn't like."

Shoels also said that Isaiah had complained of harassment shortly before the rampage, but was told by someone that those problems didn't exist at Columbine. She said she encouraged Isaiah to stay at the high school, something she now regrets.

Shari Schnurr, mother of critically wounded student Val Schnurr, said her daughter told her there was bullying at Columbine, including harassment of students because of their race and religion.

Later during October 2000 Colorado Attorney General Ken Salazar said that 5 percent of Colorado's high school students stay home once a month because they fear bullying. That finding emerged from Salazar's Safe Communities-Safe Schools Initiative, which attempted to interview students, educators, law enforcement officials, and social workers in Colorado's 176 school districts.

"When we talk about wanting to increase achievement in schools, you can't have learning and achievement in our schools if the kids are afraid to come to school," said Salazar. He reported that bullying was a problem in both small rural schools and bigger urban schools like Columbine.

I think bullying has always been around and probably always will be around. I was bullied when I was a kid. Most of the schools I attended were small, but I think the bigger the school, the less security a kid feels. In a smaller school you get to know everybody, and there are people to whom you can turn to come to your aid. In a big school like Columbine—which has 1,600 to 1,700 students—it is easy to get lost in the shuffle.

In the last chapter, we talked about how some schools have become places where people are reluctant to talk about right and wrong. When I was a kid, if teachers saw someone bullying someone else, they would step in and discipline the troublemakers. Today, some teachers say they are afraid to intervene because they don't feel they have the authority or respect to enforce that kind of discipline.

One thing that appears to be the same in all schools is that bullying usually results from feelings of inferiority on the part of the bully. That may surprise some people, who think bullies are strong, powerful people. But if you read what Eric Harris said before he died, you will see that he felt that he was picked on by some of the students at Columbine. This contributed to the anger and hatred he felt toward others at the school.

I hope that reading this book will make more young people willing to stand up to bullies—not with anger or hatred, but with kindness and compassion.

A Rule to Live By

People around the world say they believe in the golden rule. Every major religion has its own way of expressing the rule, but in the West, Jesus' words are known best: "Do unto others as you would have them do unto you." Or as Jewish scholar Rabbi Hillel put it, "That which displeases you do not do to another. That is the whole law; the rest is commentary."

But is the golden rule really a practical way to change the world? Martin Luther King Jr. thought it was, and he followed this rule in his life. Many other heroes of history have made it a foundation of their personal values and actions.

King was a revolutionary, but unlike many others, he didn't use violence to attack his enemies. He used love. In fact, King was a divinity student when he heard a lecture about Mahatma Gandhi, whose faith-based, nonviolent, passive resistance transformed the nation of India. Both King and Gandhi demonstrated that the golden rule can be a powerful tool for creating a chain reaction.

But it's not just the Mother Teresas, Martin Luther Kings, or Gandhis who can start these ripple effects. Ordinary people like you and me can make a huge difference if we simply dare to believe that we can. Clifton Bushnell is not well known, but he was someone who practiced the golden rule in a small way that made a big difference in my life.

I remember the day I was "rescued" by Clifton. I was a skinny, big-eared ten-year-old kid, living near a small town called Kinder, Louisiana. There were a couple of bullies at my school who started picking on me one day. I remember the terror that rose up in me when I realized I was cornered. Then suddenly, Clifton, who was a year or so older than I, walked up and stopped the harassment. From that moment on, Clifton became one of my heroes.

I was able to see Clifton recently when I spoke at the civic center auditorium in Lake Charles, Louisiana. I told him before the meeting that when I was a kid, he had been one of my heroes. He seemed puzzled as to why. I'm sure he doesn't remember "saving me," but it was an act of kind bravery that I shall never forget! After my speech about Rachel's life and death, Clifton came up to me with tears in his eyes and said, "I don't know why I was one of your heroes in school, but I can tell you this: you and your daughter are my heroes now!" The chain reaction had gone full circle! I was an inspiration to someone who had once been an inspiration to me.

I remember a young man named Randy Johnson from Linwood Junior High School in Shreveport, Louisiana. Randy was a very popular star football player at our school. I had just moved to Shreveport and was a new kid on the block. I will never forget how Randy went out of his way to welcome me and just say a friendly word or two every time I saw him. He'll never know how much his friendship meant to someone who felt like an outsider.

Rachel chose to live by the golden rule every day at school. She was one of the "beautiful people," but she chose to reach out to those who were not. Rachel was involved with acting and drama, but she connected with students who had different interests.

Sometimes, people ask me if I think Rachel was a hero. I always try to answer that carefully because I believe that she has become a role model for a lot of young people.

There are different definitions of what a hero is. Some people believe a hero is someone who rushes into a fire to save a child from the flames, or someone who jumps off a bridge into a roiling river to rescue someone.

Rachel didn't try to save anybody's life in dramatic ways like these. But I think she was a hero because every day she tried to think about other people. It could be something as simple as asking someone who was alone to join her for lunch. Or helping somebody with a flat tire. These aren't big-time miracles, but they are important to the people who need that kind of help at the moment.

Another reason I think Rachel was a hero is that she was willing to pay the price for doing what she thought was right. She wasn't a cartoon superhero. She never would have made it as one of the X-Women. But Rachel was a hero, and you can be a hero too.

From Hidden Hero to Sudden Superstar

There's another hero who reminds me of Rachel, and like Rachel, this young girl is someone most of us never would have heard of if it hadn't been for the way she died.

Anne Frank was born to a Jewish family in Frankfurt, Germany, on June 12, 1929. Five years later, her family moved to Amsterdam. It was there that Anne received a diary as a present for her thirteenth birthday, the diary for which so many of us remember Anne Frank today.

In 1942, the family went into hiding in a desperate attempt to avoid being rounded up by the Nazis. For the next two years, Anne wrote down everything that happened to her in her diary. As one writer put it, "She became the most memorable figure to emerge from World War II—besides Hitler, of course, who also proclaimed his life and his beliefs in a book."

"I hope that you will be a great support and comfort to me," Frank wrote in her beloved book. Later, she wrote, "I want to be useful or give pleasure to people around me who yet don't really know me. I want to go on living even after my death!"

During the two years that Anne, her sister, and her mother and father hid from the Nazis, she poured her heart into her words. One moving passage records her search for meaning at a time when evil seemed to be winning:

I simply can't build up my hopes on a foundation consisting of confusion, misery and death. I see the world gradually being turned into a wilderness; I hear the ever approaching thunder, which will destroy us too; I can feel the sufferings of millions; and yet, if I look up into the heavens, I think that it will all come right, that this cruelty will end, and that peace and tranquility will return again . . . I must uphold my ideals, for perhaps the time will come when I shall be able to carry them out.

We probably wouldn't have ever heard of Anne Frank if she had lived to be eighty years old. But she died a horrible death from typhus in the Bergen-Belsen concentration camp in 1945. Two years later, her father, Otto, who miraculously survived, published *Anne Frank: The Diary of a Young Girl,* and people both young and old have been reading about the faith and courage of this remarkable girl ever since.

The world would probably never have known who Rachel Scott was if she hadn't died at Columbine, but her acts of kindness became amplified through her death as a challenge to an entire generation of young people to make a difference with their lives!

None of us knows when we will die or how. All we can control is how we are going to live each and every moment that has been given to us. How do you want to use this precious gift of life? My prayer is that you accept the challenge to live a life of compassion and kindness. In this way, your life can create a ripple effect that will have a positive impact on everyone around you.

"I Refuse to Be a Victim"

Shortly after the tragedy at Columbine, a sixteen-year-old Littleton student named Jayson Martin wrote the following message and posted it on the Internet:

I am 16. I'm just like any other teenager. I get up every morning, go to school and come home every night. Nothing special, nothing extravagant. I'm no better than anyone else, I'm no less than anyone else. I have the same hopes, the same fears, the same questions, and the same daydreams. There are people like me in every state, in every city, in every school and in every classroom.

This morning 15 students, just like me, got up, got dressed and went to school. Some, like me, were running late, some early, some worried about the test they had first period, some were daydreaming about the cute girl that had the locker right next to theirs, some were thinking about the friend they had gotten in a fight with the night before, some were giggling with each other about the substitute with the big bright red wig. But not one of these students, just like me, was worried about walking into that school—the school they walk into every other Monday through Friday for nine months out of the year—and being shot at.

But there is a difference between these 15 students and me—I came home after school. I will be able to go on that date Friday, and pass the test, and graduate, and I am still alive.

I asked God, "Why? Why do bad things happen?" As much as I wanted a straightforward answer from Him, I didn't get one; and I know I won't, but I did get something else. I got a feeling deep down in my heart that says, "I can move mountains." And I have some mountains to move. I have no idea how to solve this problem. I have no idea what has gone wrong in the heads of so many of my peers, and I don't know how to stop it. I'm sure going to try.

Today I was saddened by what happened. I was scared and I was confused, but most of all, I was ashamed. I am ashamed. I am ashamed of my generation, of my classmates, of my friends and of myself. These shootings were done by kids my own age. Kids that you pass on the street, kids with friends, and kids with families. The kids that died are the same. These kids that were killed are innocent victims. They did not deserve to die and nothing can ever come close to making what happened justifiable.

Those who ignore this, as I have, for the past however many years, are those that I am also ashamed of. What has to happen? Does it have to happen to your family, to your kids, to your friends, to your life to open your eyes? Are you still going to wait? I'm not. I refuse to watch this happen anymore. I refuse to be a victim. I don't know how I am supposed to change the world, but I will. I am not going to stand by any longer and watch my generation flush society down the toilet. The streets aren't safe, parks aren't safe, homes aren't safe, and now schools aren't safe. There is something wrong with this picture, and I feel sorry for those that don't see it. But most of all, I pity those that do but choose to ignore it. I am making a vow to myself to stand up against it, to make a difference, and I pray I am not alone.

I would like everyone to please say a prayer for the safety of everyone who was involved in this terrible tragedy. It is something that has hurt me and my friends. Let us come together and pray that this tragedy ends soon.

Jayson's message holds a challenge for all of us. What are we going to do with the world we have received, filled as it often is with sadness and tragedy?

Like Jayson, I have taken a vow to make things better. I want to start a ripple effect with my life. Will you join us?

4
Rachel's Code for Living and Giving

Bethanee, there's a piece of paper here under Rachel's bed!"

I was calling out to Rachel's oldest sister, my oldest daughter. It was May of 1999—three weeks after Rachel's sudden and shocking death—and we were going through the process of sorting through some of Rachel's things.

It had been a difficult period for all of us. We loved Rachel and missed her deeply. We missed her smile and her energy. As we looked through some of her possessions, we half expected her to show up and say, "Hey, guys."

Rachel's basement room wasn't big. It barely had room for a bed, a small desk, and a dresser, leaving a little bit of room left for a patch of carpet. The room was full of candles she would burn to provide a warm atmosphere and a pleasant scent. She also had a few stuffed animals that made the room look like a small zoo. Like many young women her age, she had decorated her walls with photos of friends and posters from school activities.

In the weeks since her death, we had already begun to uncover Rachel's journals. These were the various notebooks into which she regularly wrote her thoughts, her prayers, and various poems and songs she would compose. As we opened these journals and read her writings, we were amazed by the maturity and depth we found in their pages.

But we had failed to look closely under her bed, where one sheet of paper had evidently slipped out of her notebook and found a hiding place in the shadows.

Bethanee and I had already been weeping together as we shared memories of Rachel while looking at items that she had left behind in the small sanctuary of her room. And now we had discovered another personal artifact that would provide an even deeper revelation into the heart of this wonderful young woman who had brought light to our lives for the past seventeen years.

The paper was actually a two-page essay that was stapled together in the upper left-hand corner. The title at the top was "My Ethics, My Codes of Life," written by "Rachel Scott, period 5." In the upper right hand of the first page, Rachel's teacher had written in a flowing hand, "You express yourself w/a sense of voice and originality—solid organization as well. I enjoyed reading this."

When we sat down on the corner of the bed to read the essay together, we could see why this teacher had given a perfect grade.

I would like you to take a minute to read Rachel's essay. During the rest of this chapter and for much of the rest of this book, I will be talking about Rachel's code of life and will also try to help you develop your own code of life.

As you read Rachel's essay, think about the values that make up the core of her code.

"My Ethics, My Codes of Life"

by Rachel Scott, period 5

Ethics vary with environment, circumstances, and culture. In my own life, ethics play a major role. Whether it was because of the way I was raised, the experiences I've had, or just my outlook on the world and the way things should be. My biggest aspects of ethics include being honest, compassionate, and looking for the best and beauty in everyone.

I have been told repeatedly that I trust people too easily, but I find that when I put my faith and trust in people when others would not dare to, they almost never betray me. I would hope that people would put the same faith in me. Trust and honesty is an investment you put in people; if you build enough trust in them and show yourself to be honest, they will do the same in you. I value honesty so much, and it is an expectation I have of myself. I will put honesty before the risk of humiliation, before selfishness, and before anything less worthy of the Gospel truth. Even in being honest and trustworthy, I do not want to come off cold and heartless. Compassion and honesty go hand in hand, if enough of each is put into every situation. I admire those who trust and are trustworthy.

Compassion is the greatest form of love that humans have to offer. According to Webster's Dictionary, compassion means a feeling of sympathy for another person's misfortune. My definition of compassion is forgiving, loving, helping, leading, and showing mercy for others. I have this theory that if one person can go out of their way to show compassion, then it will start a chain reaction of the same. People will never know how far a little kindness can go.

It wasn't until recently that I learned that the first and the second and the third impressions can be deceitful of what kind of person someone is. For example, imagine you had just met someone, and you speak with them three times on brief, everyday conversations. They come off as a harsh, cruel, stubborn, and ignorant person. You reach your judgment based on just these three encounters. Let me ask you something: Did you ever ask them what their goal in life is, what kind of past they came from, did they experience love, did they experience hurt, did you look into their soul and not just at their appearance? Until you know them and not just their "type," you have no right to shun them. You have not looked for their beauty, their good. You have not seen the light in their eyes. Look hard enough and you will always find a light, and you can even help it grow, if you don't walk away from those three impressions first.

I am sure that my codes of life may be very different from yours, but how do you know that trust, compassion, and beauty will not make this world a better place to be in and this life a better one to live? My codes may seem like a fantasy that can never be reached, but test them for yourself, and see the kind of effect they have in the lives of people around you. You just may start a chain reaction.

What Is Your Code of Life?

There is an old saying that goes something like this: If you're not sure where you're going, any path is as good as another.

What surprises me is to see that many people, no matter what their age, seem pretty directionless. By that I don't mean that they get in their cars and drive around in circles. In fact, nobody I know does that. Just about everyone seems to know, for example, how to get from home to the store, or from the store back home.

But when it comes to their lives, many people are directionless, and they don't even know it. As a result, they go one direction in life for a little while, until they change their minds, or someone influences them, and they go off in another direction.

Rachel wasn't like that. As you can see from her essay, she had strong beliefs and values about herself, about people, and about the world. These beliefs and values influenced her direction and gave her life a sense of meaning and purpose.

One of the things I would like you to do as you are reading this chapter is to think about the direction of your own life. As you think, ask yourself these questions:

- How do I feel about what I've accomplished thus far in life?

- What do I hope to accomplish during the next five years?

- Suppose I knew I was going to die six months from today. How would I spend the remaining six months of my life?

- Suppose I was to die suddenly, like Rachel did. What would people say about me? What kind legacy would I leave? What kind of ripple effect or chain reaction would I have started with my life?

Crucial Choices

In the hours after the Columbine killings, young people all over the world logged onto the Internet and exchanged their views about the tragedy. The following on-line essay, which was supposedly written by a Columbine student, was copied and posted thousands of times.

I like the essay because it is passionate, because it speaks about the spiritual issues at the heart of Columbine and many other problems in our world, and because it raises important questions about the choices we make and their impact on our world.

The paradox of our time in history is that we have taller buildings, but shorter tempers; wider freeways, but narrower viewpoints; we spend more, but have less; we buy more, but enjoy it less.

We have bigger houses and smaller families; more conveniences, but less time; we have more degrees, but less sense; more knowledge, but less judgment; more experts, but less solutions; more medicine, but less wellness.

We have multiplied our possessions, but reduced our values.
We talk too much, love too seldom, and hate too often.
We've learned how to make a living, but not a life;
We've added years to life, not life to years.
We've been all the way to the moon and back, but have trouble
    crossing the street to meet the new neighbor.
We've conquered outer space, but not inner space;
we've cleaned up the air, but polluted the soul;
we've split the atom, but not our prejudice.
We have higher incomes, but lower morals;
we've become long on quantity, but short on quality.
These are the times of tall men, and short character;
    steep profits, and shallow relationships.
These are the times of world peace, but domestic warfare;
    more leisure, but less fun; more kinds of food, but less
    nutrition.

These are days of two incomes, but more divorce;
of fancier houses, but broken homes.
It is a time when there is much in the show window and nothing
in the stockroom;
a time when technology can bring this letter to you,
and a time when you can choose either to forward this message
and make a difference . . .
or just hit delete.

Every day, each one of us is challenged by hundreds of choices, such as whether or not to forward that computer message. There are simple decisions, such as, "Am I going to wear black socks or brown socks or one of each?" And there are more complicated questions, such as, "How do I want to live my life today?"

The question about the socks probably won't make much difference in the world (unless you are a fashion model, in which case other people might try to imitate your choice in colors), but many of the more important questions you will make will have deeper and longer lasting consequences for your life and possibly for the lives of other people around you.

Two Paths

I've already talked elsewhere in this book about how Rachel and Eric Harris chose different paths in their lives, but I think it's an idea worth revisiting because it is so important.

Rachel wrote her essay about her code of life in March 1999, just one month before the Columbine tragedy took her life. Months later, I made a shocking discovery. While Rachel was writing this essay, Eric Harris, the Columbine killer who police reports say shot Rachel to death outside the school, was using a video camera to record his own and decidedly darker code of ethics.

Looking straight into a video camera lens and cradling the gun that would later cause so much death and destruction, Eric made the following statement:

> We need a [expletive] kick-start—we need to get a chain reaction going here! It's going to be like Doom [the video game] man, after the bombs explode. That [expletive] shotgun [kisses the gun] straight out of Doom.

Here were two young people who lived in the same city. They were born just days apart. They lived in comfortable houses just miles apart. They had attended some of the same classes in school. They died just a few feet apart on the same day. And they recorded their respective codes of ethics just one month before their deaths. Their challenge was to start a chain reaction! They knew that their thoughts, words, attitudes, and actions would cause repercussions or ripples that would continue forever!

Eric Harris certainly started several chain reactions. Not only did he kill innocent people at Columbine High School, he kick-started a number of "copycat" school shootings over the next year. He also knew, and predicted, that there would be a clamor for more gun control laws after the tragedy. His challenge to start a chain reaction initiated not only more tragedies, but also much debate and political posturing on such issues as gun control and police procedures concerning school shootings. His chain reaction caused death, suffering, mourning, anger, accusations, lawsuits, political debate, and more negative repercussions.

Meanwhile, Rachel's chain reaction, which was inspired by her own code of ethics, has created an entirely different set of results.

Both young people knew what they wanted to do and went about doing it with all their energy. Both also said that someday the world would know who they were.

Looking back on all of this now, I am amazed at how tremendous things can be set in motion by small beginnings. We really do start a chain reaction through our actions, attitudes, and words.

The question we need to think about is this one: What kind of chain reaction will our lives inspire?

Creating a Code That Fits

Have you ever noticed how many different kinds of people there are in the world? Sometimes the diversity in the human race seems mind-boggling, but usually, I find it reassuring. Each one of us has a unique set of experiences, attitudes, abilities, and skills that make us who we are.

Even more exciting, our unique experiences, attitudes, abilities, and skills enable us to do things that nobody else on the planet can do. And that is a good thing because the world needs each one of us. We all have important roles to play in the drama of life.

I think all of us have self-doubts at times. There is always someone out there who is bigger, better looking, faster, or smarter than we are. Sometimes I have been acutely aware of my failures and inabilities. I have realized that there are people more capable and more worthy than I, who can do far more than I ever could. At times like that I am reminded of something President Teddy Roosevelt said many years ago:

It is not the critic that counts nor the man who points out how the strong man stumbled or where the doer of deeds could have done them better. The credit belongs to the man who is actually in the arena; whose face is marred by dust and sweat and blood; who strives valiantly . . . ; who knows the great enthusiasms, the great devotions, and spends himself in a worthy cause; who, at his best, knows the triumph of high achievement; and who, at his worst, if he fails, at least fails while daring greatly, so that his place shall never be with those cold and timid souls who know neither victory nor defeat!

There was a point in my life when I had withdrawn from the fray. I was in a self-pitying, survival mode. Several years before Rachel's death I reentered the arena of life and vowed to make a difference wherever I could. I will never again measure myself against others. I will simply strive to do the best I can with what God puts in my path.

I dare you to take Rachel's challenge and start a chain reaction.

Regardless of your education, your age, your looks, your weight, or your intelligence, you can make a difference.

If we measure ourselves against the super athletes, the top movie stars, the brilliant scientists, or the great orators, we will always feel inferior and insignificant. Don't even play that game! All you should expect from yourself is to do your best with what you have. You will find your place when you simply begin to do what is put before you.

People refer to this as fulfilling one's "calling." I am not called to swim a mile in less than fifteen minutes or design the world's tallest building. I would meet with failure if I attempted either of those activities.

Although I don't claim to be the world's greatest public speaker or writer, I feel this is what I have been called to do right now. I didn't ask to be connected to one of the thirteen people who would be killed at Columbine, but I am. As a result, part of what I feel I am called to do with my life right now is to speak and write about how all of us can take the experience of Columbine and learn something from it.

Rachel was the same way. There were times when she felt insecure and compared to herself other people. She experienced periods of uncertainty and self-doubt. On the other hand, she had a confidence that was deeper than all the doubts. She believed that God had made her the way she was, and that was OK. Rather than focusing on her problems and inabilities, she made a realistic assessment of her unique experiences, attitudes, abilities, and skills and decided to use them in ways that would best benefit the world.

Rachel wasn't without her nagging doubts and fears, but in the long run, she was comfortable with who she was. And that enabled her to reach out to others from a position of confidence instead of always manipulating other people to make herself feel better.

I particularly noticed that during the last two years of her life, Rachel really figured out who she was and functioned out of that knowledge. Her goals grew out of it. Just about everything Rachel did flowed out of who she was and what she valued. These things helped her find her purpose or calling in the world.

Sometimes, if we try to copy what other people around us do or think, we look like pretenders. Instead, we have to find what it is that we can do and do it.

Rachel's code of life reflected who she was and what she believed. Your code of life should do the same. Your goal in life should not be based on trying to copy what other people are doing.

You have your own role to play and your own skills to work with. These unique abilities, combined with your own set of personally meaningful values and beliefs, will give you a strong foundation for a life full of living and giving.

I'm not sure Rachel ever actually wrote a mission statement, but she did write some thoughts about her purpose in her journal. Here's what she wrote:

> Things untold
> Things unseen
> One day all these things
> Will come to me.
>
> Life of meaning
> Life of hope
> Life of significance
> Is mine to cope.
>
> I have a purpose
> I have a dream
> I have a future
> So it seems

I recently wrote my own personal mission statement:

I want my life to be productive in motivating and educating millions of young people as a result of Rachel's life and legacy. I also want to be a mentor to a handful of future leaders.

I met with some friends, and we formed a mission statement for Chain Reaction, the organization dedicated to spreading Rachel's story and her ideals.

With the backdrop of the Columbine tragedy, we intend to inspire, educate, and motivate young people to start a lasting chain reaction through extreme acts of deliberate kindness.

Perhaps using these as examples, you can write a mission statement of your own that reflects your values and your purpose in life.

Choosing Your Habits

When people use the term *habits,* they are often talking about bad habits, like the person who constantly complains, or someone who never fulfills the promises he has made.

It is also possible to have good habits, and these can help us have a positive impact in our lives. In fact, I would like this book to become a habit-forming book, in the good sense.

Some people have said that a habit is the accumulation of a bunch of really small choices. Another way to look at it is that a habit forms a character, and a character forms a life, and a life forms a destiny. So all of these things are linked.

In that sense, because all of these seemingly small things add up to a pattern of behaviors that will be either positive or negative in their cumulative effect, there are no little deeds and actions, or little thoughts and words.

As I stated in an earlier chapter, a ripple effect starts when you drop a stone into the water. Though it seems logical to think that only the big boulders have any real impact in life, the truth is that the little pebbles start ripples, too, and no matter what size the stone, these ripples spread out farther and farther every second.

You may be at a particular point in your life when you think you are not of much importance and your decisions are of no particular significance, but that is not true.

The values you embrace, the choices you make, and the actions you take are going to set in motion a whole series of consequences that may have a profound effect on your life and the lives of others around you.

Don't you think it would be a good idea to choose your values and your actions carefully, so the consequences that flow from them are ones that you will feel good about?

Correcting Your Course

It's a good thing to have a solid set of values and a clear direction in life. But you also need to be flexible and willing to make adjustments along the way as you undergo some of life's little surprises.

Imagine for a moment that you are trying to sail across the ocean from Virginia to Ireland. You have a lot of ocean to cross, so you decide to use your compass to figure out where you want to go and you set your rudder so the boat goes in the right direction.

That is a good start, but all kinds of things can happen while you're sailing. The waves and currents may change direction, and this will have an impact on the direction of your boat. The winds may also change your course. If you don't take out your compass during your trip and use it to adjust your rudder, you might wind up at the North Pole or the South Pole instead of landing safely in Ireland.

Life is the same way. It would be an understatement to say that I don't look at things the way as I did when I was fifteen years old. When I was a teenager, I felt life was going to last forever. Now I know that is not the case. I may not be able to achieve all the

Grandma Moses was close to death before she realized that her calling in life was to create beautiful works of art.

Many people don't really find out what their real niche is until they have traveled down dozens of wrong roads and arrived at hundreds of seeming dead ends. But if these people hadn't tried so many different things along the way, they never would have found their true callings.

Rachel dreamed big, and she put her dreams into action day by day. Don't let the fear of failure keep you from finding your true purpose in life. Try things out, and when they don't work the way you thought they would, change your course and try again. Only by repeated trials and errors will you find your purpose and learn to give the gift that only you can give to the world.

Learning from Rachel's Example

The part of Rachel's essay most important to me is the sentence in which she wrote down her five key values: "My definition of compassion is forgiving, loving, helping, leading, and showing mercy for others."

In the following five chapters, I will discuss each of these values in detail. Perhaps by seeing how she tried to put her values into action, you can gain insight and inspiration that will help you do something similar with your life.

5

Forgiving

Columbine has radically changed the lives of everyone it has touched. Parents, friends, relatives, schoolteachers, law enforcement personnel, survivors, and others have been permanently altered by what they have gone through here in Littleton.

Many of the victims' family members were suddenly thrust into the national spotlight. Our private griefs and public comments were broadcast around the world.

One of the things that startled me was the reaction I received when I responded to questions about my feelings toward Eric Harris and Dylan Klebold, the two troubled young men who unleashed the Columbine tragedy. When I stated that I had chosen to forgive the killers, I frequently saw shock and dismay on people's faces.

Forgiveness was one of the most important parts of Rachel's code of ethics. Ironically, I was called on to forgive the two people who caused me immeasurable grief.

Afternoon TV talk show host Rosie O'Donnell heard some of my comments about forgiving Eric and Dylan. Later, she talked about this experience in an October 1999 *McCall's* article titled "Rosie for Real."

Here is part of that article, featuring two questions an interviewer asked Rosie:

Q: What do you teach your kids?

Rosie: Love, kindness, compassion. I think of Columbine again. The father of Rachel Scott, one of the victims, said he had no hatred in his heart for the boys who did it. That just brought me to my knees, because imagine that kind of grace in the face of such darkness. The fact that light came through in this horrible situation was just devastating to me. It devastated me spiritually, more than any event that I can recall happening recently in my life. It was so hard to get through it. You don't want to make it personal. It did not happen to me. I am not one of the people who is suffering with the loss, but I think of what it did to the soul of the nation.

Q: Are you a spiritual person?

Rosie: I think the tragedy at Columbine gave me a spirituality I had never been faced with before. I think I needed God's help to get over it. I saw things. It changed my perspective. People have said to me since then, "Did something happen to you that you're not telling us about?" Someone even asked my publicist if my mother had been shot years ago. I don't know why it affected me the way it did. It got to the point where I didn't think I could do my show because I couldn't stop crying. The first thing I thought of was that the only thing worse than being one of the parents of those dead children was being the parent of one of the children who killed them. I don't know why that went into my head. It was just such a wake-up call. There's a part in the Mass where the priest holds up the Host and says "This is the Lamb of God who takes away the sins of the world. Happy are those who are called to his supper." I wonder if it was an appeal to try to do something. You have to ask yourself, did it summon your soul, and in what way will you work to try to prevent things like this from ever happening again?

Rosie is not the only person who has been shaken to the core of her being following Columbine. Millions of people have struggled to come to grips with this tragedy. Out of the soul-searching, sadness, and sorrow, I think one of the lasting lessons is Rachel's belief that we must forgive one another.

The Strength to Forgive

In her Code of Ethics, Rachel wrote, "My definition of compassion is forgiving, loving, helping, leading, and showing mercy for others." She mentioned forgiving first, but for some people forgiveness is a difficult thing to put into practice.

Some people think forgiving someone who has hurt you is a weak thing to do. They believe it is similar to giving up or giving in. I see forgiveness as an act of the heart that requires a strength beyond my own.

There are many ways to define *forgiveness*. Philosophers and theologians have been arguing over definitions for centuries. I think of forgiveness simply as letting go. It is an inward letting go my emotions of anger and bitterness that often arise when I feel I've been injured.

Writer Frederick Buechner developed his own definition of *for-giveness*:

> To forgive somebody is to say one way or another, "You have done something unspeakable, and by all rights I should call it quits between us. Both my pride and my principles demand no less. However, although I make no guarantees that I will be able to for-get what you've done and though we may both carry the scars for life, I refuse to let it stand between us." (*Wishful Thinking* [New York: Harper & Row, 1973], pp. 28–29)

Giving in to anger instead of forgiving seem a natural enough thing to do, but there are so many downsides to this approach. Refusal to forgive can lead to bitterness and the desire for revenge.

I believe lack of forgiveness can be like a cancer that will even-tually eat away at our insides and will destroy the people around us. Let me give you an example of why I think that.

The Disabling Power of Resentment

Following Columbine, I have had the opportunity to speak to groups of people all over the world. I recently spoke at a large community gathering in Mississippi where I met a young woman who was disabled by resentment.

A drunk driver ran into the woman's sister when the sister was in high school twelve years earlier. She had been a cheerleader and had felt that her entire life lay ahead of her. Suddenly, she knew she would spend the rest of her life disabled and dependent on the use of a wheelchair.

Perhaps surprisingly, the victim chose to forgive the man who put her in the wheelchair, but not all members of her family were so forgiving.

Her parents struggled with sorrow and sadness for three years and finally decided to let go of the hurt and bitterness they felt toward the drunk driver.

Further, these caring parents decided to help their daughter create a new and meaningful life in the context of her limitations. They helped her learn how to string beads together, and today she has developed this into a solid little business. They also encouraged her to take up writing, and today she writes for the local newspaper and is well respected in the local community.

Everything seemed to be looking up for this young lady, who was finding creative ways of transcending bitterness with "betterness." But her sister didn't feel the same way.

Following the accident, the young woman's sister had grown bitter. Her whole life became obsessed with her anger toward the man who had done this to her sister. It affected her physical appearance, making her once happy face look tight and pinched. It affected everybody around her, as her former pleasant manner was replaced by a brittle nastiness. For twelve long years, this sister had grown ever more unhappy and isolated.

This sister was in Mississippi the night I spoke about forgiveness to a crowd of nearly ten thousand people. Many people were moved by my comments, including the sister, who came up to me the next morning before I left town.

She told me her whole sad story and how she had reached a point of decision.

"Last night," she said, "I decided that if you can forgive someone who killed your daughter, I have to be able to forgive someone who injured my sister. Now, for the first time I have made a decision to let go, and when I did, it was like a whole fountain broke inside of me. I cried all night long. This may sound strange, but I've decided to really forgive and to let go of the whole situation, and already I feel a change. I feel like a burden has been lifted."

As I headed back to Denver that morning, I wondered at length which of these two young women had been the most disabled by that accident twelve years ago, the young girl in the wheelchair or her sister? As I thought about it, I decided that the real disabled person was the sister who had been emotionally deformed by giving in to negative thoughts and feelings for more than a decade.

Don't get me wrong. Forgiveness is not a cure-all for everything that is wrong with the world, and I'm not guaranteeing that forgiveness will always create this kind of amazing overnight transformation. I do know, however, that letting go can change any of us. Loosening our grip on hurts, jealousies, anger, and desire for retribution can open a place in our hearts that has been closed, enabling us to live and love again.

Sipping from a Cup of Poison

Just about every religious tradition in the world speaks about the importance of forgiveness. Psychiatrists and counselors are talking about it more and more as they see people who become broken and twisted inside because they harbor feelings of bitterness and anger.

Being angry is like taking tiny sips from a big cup of poison. I have a bottle of weed killer in my garage. The side of the bottle is covered with all kinds of big, bold warnings saying that I shouldn't drink it or even breathe its fumes. So I do not, because I know if I open up that bottle and take a big drink, I will get very, very sick, and soon after that I will be very, very dead.

But suppose I thought I could find a way to ignore these warnings? Suppose I thought the poison tasted good, and instead of taking a big drink, I took small sips—one every day for the next few months? I may have thought I was avoiding the effects of the poison, but poisons have a way of adding up and killing you in the long run.

It is the same way with bitterness, anger, and resentment. Over time these feelings build up and poison our lives. We may not die overnight, but slowly and surely, these destructive emotions are tearing us apart inside. These emotions are like poison that, unless dealt with properly, can destroy our lives.

That is why, over a period of many, many years, I have developed a habit of forgiveness. I said in the last chapter that a habit is a behavior that a person chooses to repeat until it becomes his natural response. This is the approach I've taken with forgiveness. The Columbine tragedy wasn't the first time I forgave anybody. I had been developing a habit of trying to forgive people for a long, long time. That's why I was able to forgive after Rachel was gunned down.

When that crucial test came, it was not that difficult to choose the right response; it was a choice I had made before. Developing my habit of forgiveness allowed me to consider forgiving not the right response, but the only response. Not to choose the right thing is to choose death.

I know Rosie O'Donnell was amazed that I could forgive my daughter's killers, but I don't really view it as a noble thing on my part. It's simply that I knew what unforgiveness could do to hurt me. I have seen what it has done to other people, and I have also seen what it did to me.

So I chose to pray for the families of those boys. I chose to let go of any potential anger or bitterness. Then reading what my daughter wrote about forgiveness reinforced what I was feeling. In her code of ethics essay, she said that forgiving is one way to start a positive chain reaction.

Sure, there are times when practicing forgiveness is difficult. Sometimes it is an easy choice to forgive someone who has wronged me, and other times it is a tough choice. But either way, forgiveness is the only good choice because the consequence of not forgiving is suffering, inflicted upon ourselves and those around us.

The best proof I can offer you of this truth is the lives of Eric Harris and Dylan Klebold. I believe that a lack of forgiveness may be at the core of the troubles they had.

The videotapes they left behind make this truth pretty clear. As I watched the tapes they made before their killing spree, I became convinced that these two boys didn't know how to let go. Everything that ever happened to them became fuel for their fury. In this case, we can plainly see that unforgiveness doesn't just affect us; it affects others and possibly even generations after us.

It's like the traditional feuds between the Hatfields and the McCoys. This is a story we joke about, but we know it speaks the truth. Unforgiveness is a powerful poison, and it can be passed from one generation to another.

Another School, Another Shooting

One of the saddest things about America in our time is that when somebody says, "There's been a shooting at a school," someone else will say, "What, another one?" There should never have been a single school shooting in this country. Preying on innocent children is wrong, wrong, wrong.

Please don't misunderstand me. Just because I am saying that we should forgive doesn't mean that I don't draw clear distinctions between what's wrong and what's right. What Eric and Dylan did was wrong. It was evil. Had they lived rather than taking their own lives, I would have been there to prosecute them for their crime and to see to it that they wouldn't have the opportunity to do something like this ever again. I believe in forgiveness, but I also believe that people should pay the consequences of their actions.

Forgiveness doesn't mean I call evil good, or pretend that bad things didn't happen. Forgiveness simply means that I refuse to harbor bitterness, anger, resentment, and other feelings that are going to destroy me if I hold them.

The way I look at it, if we do not choose to forgive, we are going to be victimized twice: once by the person who did something to hurt us and a second time by the unforgiveness itself.

I came across an example while I was in Georgia speaking to another large crowd of people whose faces showed that they had been touched by Rachel's life and message. After the meeting, a man spoke to my wife. She called me over, and I talked to him for a while. This man's son had been shot and injured in the high school shooting in Conyers, Georgia, one year earlier. That shooting didn't have any fatalities, but there were some serious injuries. The man's son, a football player at the school, had been hit by one of the shooter's bullets.

The father admitted that, though his son had let go of the whole situation, he had not been able to, and it was tying him in knots. "You just talked tonight about unforgiveness disabling people, and I've been disabled for a year," he told me. "I've just been angry and uptight. My whole life and everything in it have been affected. I know I've got to choose to let go."

Sometimes letting go takes a lot of strength. For this father, who had struggled with feelings of sadness and revenge as he saw his son struggle to recover from his injuries, letting go had seemed the last thing he could do. After a year of wallowing in his own anger, he had had enough of bitterness and had decided to let go. It's something you can do, too, if you try.

Putting Forgiveness into Action

Forgiving is not easy; it actually takes practice over a long period of time to make it a consistent part of your life.

Here are practical ideas for putting forgiveness into action in your life.

Shorten Your Enemies List

Some people walk through life with a long list of perceived enemies they want to strike back at or get even with. But life is too short to be consumed with feelings of bitterness and revenge. When you're nice and relaxed (either before you fall to sleep at night, or perhaps after talking a long walk in the park), think of some of the people you are angry with, and forgive them one by one. If you find yourself getting angry with these people all over again, forgive them all over again. Only by continued action can you free yourself from the disabling effects of unforgiveness.

Be Forgiving in Both Big Things and Small Things

I don't know about you, but it is terribly easy for me to experience a sudden flash of anger at someone who pulls in front of me in traffic. I have never gotten out of my car and started an act of "road rage," but I have certainly felt rage in my heart any number of times. Perhaps like me, you will have to concentrate on practicing forgiveness not only in the big hurts of life but also in the small and incidental situations where anger and hurt can arise.

Seek Forgiveness from Others

I've got some startling news for you: it is not just other people who hurt you all the time, but you hurt others as well. Take a moment to think of situations where you have treated people unfairly. If you think there is any chance that your behavior has harmed your relationships with those individuals, go to them and seek their forgiveness as humbly and as quickly as possible. Try to be more aware of the hurtful consequences of your actions. You will be surprised by how a little more sensitivity on your part can help you avoid hurting people around you.

6
Loving

What is love? Poets and philosophers have been trying to answer that question for centuries. Although nobody has come up with a perfect definition, the search for one has inspired some of the world's best-known poems, paintings, and movies.

In her Code of Ethics, Rachel wrote, "My definition of compassion is forgiving, loving, helping, leading, and showing mercy for others."

Psychiatrist Karl Menninger said, "Love cures people, the ones who receive love and the ones who give it too."

W. Stanley Mooneyham, former president of the international organization World Vision, said, "Love talked about can be easily turned aside, but love demonstrated is irresistible."

Author Boris Pasternak wrote that "love is not weakness. It is strong. Only the sacrament of marriage can contain it."

Actor Peter Ustinov said, "Love is an act of endless forgiveness, a tender look which becomes a habit."

Psychologist Erich Fromm believed that love has a profound impact on all our lives: "Love is the only sane and satisfactory answer to the problem of human existence."

Counselor and author M. Scott Peck contrasted two types of love: "Real love is a permanently self-enlarging experience. Falling in love is not."

According to writer Simone Weil, "The love of our neighbor in all its fullness simply means being able to say to him, 'What are you going through?'"

Harry Emerson Fosdick explained the liberating power of love when he wrote, "Bitterness imprisons life; love releases it. Bitterness paralyzes life; love empowers it. Bitterness sours life; love sweetens it. Bitterness sickens life; love heals it. Bitterness blinds life; love anoints its eyes."

Fiction writer Ursula K. Le Guin said love must be dynamic, always growing and changing: "Love doesn't just sit there, like a stone; it has to be made, like bread, remade all the time, made new."

Actress Ginger Rogers said, "When two people love each other, they don't look at each other, they look in the same direction."

Theologian Paul Tillich declared, "The first duty of love is to listen."

Jewish thinker Elie Wiesel wrote, "The opposite of love is not hate, it's indifference."

The Bible says much about love. Probably one of the most important statements about love is the Old Testament command repeated later by Jesus: "Love your neighbor as yourself." The Song of Solomon tells us, "Love is as strong as death, jealousy as cruel as the grave."

C. S. Lewis, probably one of the most quotable writers of the twentieth century, said, "This is one of the miracles of love: It gives a power of seeing through its own enchantments and yet not being disenchanted."

Last of all I'll leave you with a wrong definition of *love* given in a famous movie made many years back: "Love is never having to say you're sorry." That's the worst definition of *love* I have ever heard! Love begins with saying, "I'm sorry!"

Perhaps you have thoughts of your own about what love is and what it means.

One of the most powerful episodes of the Columbine tragedy revealed love in action.

The Story Behind the Story

Cassie Bernall became one of the best-known symbols of the Columbine tragedy after stories circulated about her bravery in the face of death.

According to reports of Columbine students who survived the massacre, one of the killers pointed a gun at Cassie and asked her if she believed in God. After answering that she did, she was unceremoniously shot.

Cassie's story, which spread around the world by word of mouth, TV and newspaper reports, and the Internet, led to her being revered as a modern-day saint by religious groups all over the country. As a *Newsweek* reporter wrote, "Because of her last words, Cassie Bernall is now being hailed . . . as an authentic martyr for the faith."

Her courage and the strength of her convictions endeared her to millions of young people who did not even share her Christian beliefs. As the *Chicago Tribune* put it, "From time to time, an example of true moral heroism shows up, a case in which someone has the wisdom to recognize a moral imperative and the fortitude to act upon it. When the case involves someone as young and courageous as Cassie Bernall, it is more than heartening; it is humbling and awe-inspiring."

There is more to the Cassie Bernall story than these articles reveal. In her best-selling book *She Said Yes*, Cassie's mother, Misty, described in harrowing detail Cassie's downward spiral into depression, her experimentation with witchcraft, her thoughts about suicide, and her secret desire—expressed in letters to a friend—to murder her own parents.

"We were losing our daughter," wrote Misty, who went on to describe how Cassie "had been sliding away from us ever since sixth grade."

Fearing for their daughter's life and safety, Misty and her husband, Brad, committed themselves to rescuing her, although they knew Cassie would not like it at all.

They met with the parents of Cassie's friend, Mona, the girl to whom Cassie had written her angry letters. They went to the police to get a restraining order separating the two girls from each other. They took Cassie out of public school and enrolled her in a more strict Christian school. They had their home phone tapped so they could monitor Cassie's calls. And when old friends who had a negative influence on Cassie continued to contact her, Misty and Brad sold their house and moved to a different neighborhood.

As you might expect, Cassie initially resisted all their efforts. Although they were motivated by love for their daughter, Cassie couldn't see the love. All she could see were the restrictions on her freedom.

In time, Cassie began to change. A key point in her transformation happened when she came to believe in God—a commitment that was originally made in private but would later resound around the world. Soon, her life had new direction. No longer seeking to hurt herself or others around her, Cassie began to seek ways to help and reach out to others.

Practicing Tough Love

As Cassie's story shows, love isn't always soft and fuzzy. Sometimes love has to be tough.

Who knows what would have become of Cassie Bernall had she lived? We do know that her life was radically impacted by the love and commitment of her parents.

Misty Bernall exhibited tough love. For her, love wasn't something that was sentimental and syrupy. Rather, she loved her daughter enough to invest in her and protect her. She loved Cassie enough to confront her. This is the true nature of tough love. Her love was strong and courageous enough to reach out to another.

The simplest way I can explain this kind of love is to say that it is the kind of love most of us parents have for our children.

For example, say I have a three-year-old son who is playing in the front yard. If I love my child, I will keep a close eye on him. If he doesn't know any better than to run out to the middle of the street where he could be run over by a car, it is not loving for me to let him do what he wants. Rather, it is because I love that child that I restrain him, preventing him from putting himself in harm's way.

As our children grow older, they continually challenge the boundaries that we impose on them. If we have been good parents, we hope we have trained them to the point where they need less discipline as they grow older.

No matter who we are or where we are, when we see someone, whether a spouse, parent, or friend at school destroying himself, if we really love him, we will try to prevent him from destroying himself or others.

A Private Rage Builds

If all people exhibited the kind of tough and deeply involved love that Misty and Brad Bernall showed to Cassie, the Columbine tragedy might have never happened.

Sadly, while the Bernalls were practicing tough love with Cassie, things weren't quite so cozy in two other Denver area homes.

According to a *Denver Post* article published on November 22, 2000, titled "Friends of Killers Saw Rage Building," both friends and parents of Columbine killers Eric Harris and Dylan Klebold failed to use tough love with the young men.

The article was based on 10,937 pages of crime investigation records that were released on November 21, 2000. The records show that many people had noticed a rage building in Eric and Dylan. Coworkers had seen them explode bombs, and there had been gas fumes in their houses from bombs under construction.

I'm not trying to single out the parents for condemnation, but I am asking, Why didn't more people see any of these signs? And why didn't anyone do anything? Where was the love these boys needed?

The beginning of the *Denver Post* article summarizes the problem: "While friends saw the violent fantasies of Eric Harris and Dylan Klebold turn into an arsenal of guns and bombs, the teens' parents never suspected their sons were plotting the Columbine High School massacre."

The article goes on to detail numerous cases in which people who should have known better failed to step in and show tough love to Eric and Dylan:

In the months before the 1999 rampage, one coworker saw Harris and Klebold explode a "dry ice" bomb during their shift at a Blackjack Pizza parlor. A friend watched the teens detonate another bomb in a ditch near Chatfield Reservoir. In his bedroom, Harris also showed the friend two pipe bombs, built with instructions taken from the Internet.

But on the day of the killings, in a house rife with gasoline fumes, Wayne Harris told police he had "no reason to believe his son would be involved with such a situation." The father told police that his son's "interest in explosives and firearms was no more than you would expect from a person looking forward to joining the Marine Corps."

The Klebolds also were blindsided by their son's senseless rage.

"Mr. Klebold said he had no idea what happened or why, and indicated that Dylan was his best friend and that they spent a lot of time together," investigators wrote in an April 30 report. "The Klebolds indicated that Dylan was gentle, and was that way until the day he died."

But violent warnings already had been picked up at school. Two months before the worst school shooting in U.S. history, a teacher warned Klebold's parents that their son had written "the most vicious story I have ever read"—an account of a man dressed in black who murdered "all the popular kids." "It's just a story," Klebold told creative writing teacher Judith Kelly.

The two students maintained apparent "hit lists" of school-mates to be murdered, and a final video and tape recording described in the bluntest terms how they planned to destroy the school they so despised.

"People will die because of me. It will be a day that will be remembered forever," said Harris in a microcassette found by police in the kitchen of his home.

Later, when police began searching the Harris house, they found graduation announcements on the dining room table, and a list of people to whom they would be sent. But they also found a handwritten note, lying on the kitchen table, detailing what appeared to be an "itinerary" for the rampage at the high school.

And on a table by Harris' bed, they found what appeared to be a time line for the massacre and the number of people he intended to kill.

Nate Dykeman, a close friend of both Harris and Klebold, said he knew the two had been experimenting with explosives for more than a year. In fact, Dykeman said he helped Harris remove and store powder from fireworks in a coffee can.

Dykeman told police he saw several small bombs "sitting out in the open in his bedroom." He added that Harris once took him into the basement and knocked on a hollow area inside a window well—a hiding place, Harris told him, for bombs he must keep hidden because he'd just gotten into a juvenile diversion program to atone for his burglary of a van.

In yet another tour of the Harris home, Eric took Dykeman into his parents' bedroom closet to show him a pipe bomb his father had confiscated. Eric told him his father had put it there because he didn't know what to do with it.

Dykeman also told authorities he once saw Klebold slip several twenty-dollar bills to Blackjack coworker Phil Duran, and thought at first that he'd witnessed a drug transaction. But Klebold later told Dykeman that the money had been for a shotgun, and that Duran had earlier sold him a semiautomatic pistol.

In woods outside the Klebold's expansive home, however, police also found shotgun wads and a "small electronic device." Police found evidence of an explosion there.

The article goes on to detail other missed opportunities where people who knew the would-be killers could have stepped in and might have made a difference:

- People listed in Eric Harris's planning book—under the title "Class of '98 that should have died"—said they weren't surprised by the gunmen's actions. One said there had been rumors for two years about Harris's and Dylan Klebold's plans to blow up the school, and that school officials who were told of the allegations refused to take them seriously.

- On April 19, students saw Harris looking around outside the school library. When asked "What's up?" Harris responded, "Planning for tomorrow." The student assumed Harris was planning another video for class.

- Student Alexandrea Marsh, who was at Columbine the day of the attack, said Klebold and Harris had been angry after being ostracized by athletes and had talked about "blowing up the school," but she was under the impression they were not serious.

A Friend Loves and Cares

Just like millions of other Americans, I wish with all my heart that Harris's and Klebold's parents had been close enough to their sons to see some of the signs of turmoil and despair. I wish they had asked some questions, delved a little deeper, gotten more involved.

The same goes for the boys' friends and fellow students. I wish someone had broken through the walls by reaching out in love to these troubled teens.

In one of the journals found after Rachel's death, we discovered an entry she had written called "A Friend." Perhaps if more of us exhibited this kind of friendly concern, there would be fewer tragedies like Columbine.

A friend . . .
A friend is someone who can look into your eyes and be able to tell if you're alright or not.
A friend . . .
A friend is someone who can say something to you without you telling them anything and their words hit the spot.
A friend . . .
A friend is someone who can brighten your day with a simple smile when others try to do it with a 1000 words.
A friend . . .
A friend is someone who can reach out their hand and help you thru the hurt.
A friend . . .
A friend is someone who can help me and talk to me the way you do . . . and in you I have found a friend.

In Search of the Meaning of Love

Ancient Greek philosophers arrived at three different concepts of love:

One concept is *eros* (from which we get our word *erotic*). For the Greeks, this referred to sensual, sexual love.

The second concept, *phileo,* describes the brotherly love that can exist between true friends. The city of Philadelphia is thus known as the city of brotherly love.

Agape is the third concept of love. For many people, this is the least familiar of the three concepts. I believe it is the most important because agape describes the kind of self-giving and unconditional love that I think is most needed in our world today.

This is love in its purest form. It is sacrificial. It is giving with no expectation of return. It's the kind of love that a mother has for a child when she's willing to die to save that child. It's the kind of love a soldier has when he risks his own life to save the life of a fallen comrade. Love is not just a mushy feeling. It's a commitment.

There's a passage in the Bible (NIV) that powerfully describes this kind of selfless agape love:

> If I speak in the tongues of men and of angels, but have not love, I am only a resounding gong or a clanging cymbal.
>
> If I have the gift of prophecy and can fathom all mysteries and all knowledge, and if I have a faith that can move mountains, but have not love, I am nothing.
>
> If I give all I possess to the poor and surrender my body to the flames, but have not love, I gain nothing.
>
> Love is patient, love is kind. It does not envy, it does not boast, it is not proud.
>
> It is not rude, it is not self-seeking, it is not easily angered, it keeps no record of wrongs.
>
> Love does not delight in evil but rejoices with the truth.
>
> It always protects, always trusts, always hopes, always perseveres.
>
> Love never fails. But where there are prophecies, they will

cease; where there are tongues, they will be stilled; where there is knowledge, it will pass away.

For we know in part and we prophesy in part, but when perfection comes, the imperfect disappears.

When I was a child, I talked like a child, I thought like a child, I reasoned like a child. When I became a man, I put childish ways behind me.

Now we see but a poor reflection as in a mirror; then we shall see face to face. Now I know in part; then I shall know fully, even as I am fully known.

And now these three remain: faith, hope and love. But the greatest of these is love.

Movies About Love

People love to see movies about love. That's why films like *Pretty Woman* and *Ghost* were among the most popular films of the 1990s.

Movies can be tricky, though. Sometimes, filmgoers might expect a film to be about love and later realize it is not, while other films that you would not necessarily expect to have anything to say about the subject wind up telling us a lot about love.

Here is what I mean. The movie *American Pie* is a popular film about guys and girls and sex, but real love is surprisingly absent.

In the film, four average high school guys who are depressed about the fact that they are still virgins make a pact to remedy the problem in the remaining three weeks before their class prom. The film portrays their desperate efforts to track down willing partners and have sex. The ancient Greeks would say this film is obsessed with eros but totally ignorant of agape.

Saving Private Ryan is ostensibly about war, death, and dying, but surprisingly, the movie contains the powerful message that love isn't about what you can get for yourself but about what you can give to others.

In the Oscar-winning movie, Tom Hanks plays a World War II army captain who leads a squad of seven soldiers into enemy territory in France to find and rescue a private whose three brothers have already been killed in combat. The film's powerful battle scenes are disturbingly real, as is the movie's portrayal of heroism.

Hanks and his fellow soldiers risk their lives for the sake of a fellow soldier. In the process, they reveal more about the phileo and agape forms of love than most other films do.

Taking Time to Connect

In the real world, love is often hard to find, and ever since Columbine, thinkers, writers, and social scientists have worked overtime trying to figure out why violence erupted there and at other schools.

On the first anniversary of the tragedy, YROCK.com, a conservative political Web site, conducted a survey that asked Americans what caused the killings. The headline of a Religion News Service wire story said it all: "Poll Sees Parents, Not Guns, as Cause of Youth Violence."

According to the Religion News Service story, the poll found that Americans believe the primary cause for school shootings and youth violence is the drop in parental quality time with children, not the availability of guns.

When asked to choose from a list of possible factors that are the "greater cause of youth violence and school shootings today," 42 percent of respondents picked "the decline in quality time parents spend with their children." Thirty percent chose "the violence

they see and hear on television, movies, music and video games."
Eleven percent picked "access to guns," 10 percent chose "the lack
of good role models," and 5 percent chose "the failure of schools
to promote civility and moral values." The rest of the respondents
said they didn't know or refused to answer the question.

Asked what would have the greater influence on reducing such
violence overall, 77 percent of respondents said "teaching children
at a young age about right and wrong and respect for human life."
Twelve percent of respondents cited stricter school discipline, 10
percent chose more gun control legislation, and the rest said they
didn't know or refused to answer.

Eighty-four percent of respondents said greater parent involve-
ment in children's lives would have the most influence on specifically reducing gun violence in schools. Fourteen percent of those
surveyed said more gun control legislation would have the greatest
influence, and the rest said they didn't know or refused to answer.

Most of those surveyed said they believed recent school shootings indicate a national moral decline. Forty-eight percent said
they strongly agreed with that statement, and 32 percent said they
agreed somewhat with it.

You may not be a parent, but regardless of who you are or what
your status in life, you can spend quality time with the people
around you.

A Final Talk

I know it's a cliché to talk about "quality time," but I feel it is a
tremendously important concept. A few days before Rachel died,
she and I had one of the best conversations we had had in years. I
didn't know it at the time that this would be our last real talk.

Rachel had been out late one night and was cited for breaking the Littleton curfew, so I had to take her downtown to pay a fine. She hadn't done anything wrong, but the city is strict about its curfew, and she had violated it.

Afterward, we were sitting at the dining table. We did not purposely sit down to have a heart-to-heart talk. We just started talking, and suddenly, I found myself saying things that kind of surprised me. As I started talking, I realized that I was in the middle of a father-daughter conversation with someone who once was a little girl but had gradually become a young woman. Though her graduation was still a year away, I just felt comfortable sharing with her as an adult about all kinds of things.

I remember talking to her about wanting to spend more time with her before she graduated and went to college. I expressed my regrets for not always having been a perfect father.

I talked about how Sandy and I were looking forward to getting married and enjoying grandchildren, and that my whole life had been preparing me to be a grandpa. I'll never forget her beautiful smile as I talked about grandchildren. And then her smile faded, and she was very quiet for a little while. Rachel seemed to know she would never live long enough to have children. In fact, she had expressed that very thought to some of her close friends.

As we talked, we expressed our unconditional love to each other. I told her that just a couple of days earlier I had met with two of my close friends, John Curtis and Buz Hicks. We had poured our hearts out to each other as old friends, and I had expressed my appreciation and love for them at lunch together. I said, "Rachel, I love those two old guys unconditionally after years of fighting and friendship, but my feelings toward them can't compare to how much you mean to me."

I'll never forget her sitting there, tilting her head to one side, with a big smile on her face. I remember feeling how blessed I was to have such a beautiful, wonderful daughter, not just physically beautiful, but spiritually beautiful as well. Little did I realize at the time that I would be reliving that visit with her thousands of times. You see, it is the last time I saw Rachel alive.

As we talked, our conversation moved to a very intense level until we were both crying. We got up simultaneously and embraced at the head of the table. We stood there for a long time just hugging each other and sobbing.

I didn't know at the time that this was to be our good-bye talk, but looking back on it now, I know there was nothing left unsaid between us. It was a total openness, and I believe that God ordained that talk.

Months after Rachel had died, somebody asked me what I would want to say to her if she could come back. I thought about it and answered, "I said everything I had to say to Rachel that day. I told her exactly how I felt about her, and I told her how much I loved her. We left nothing unsaid. We left no stones unturned."

Perhaps there is someone in your life who does not know how much you love him or her. Maybe it is someone who lives in your house—a parent or brother or sister. Maybe it is a friend at school who has been there for you during some of your toughest moments. Maybe it is a teacher or a coach who has inspired you to do your best (and has not condemned you when you have not done your best).

Whoever it is, please let him know today or as soon as possible how much you love and appreciate him. You never know. It could be your last chance to tell him.

More Than a Feeling

One kind of love nearly everybody is familiar with is puppy love, which is the excited romantic love that makes many young people feel as if they are on top of the world. I do not know about you, but my experiences of puppy love did not last. I cannot even remember some of the girls I had crushes on in elementary school because those infatuations did not last.

But real love lasts. It endures conflict and disagreements. It survives the passage of months and years. Love is not just a mushy feeling; it is a commitment. It is the kind of commitment that leads to action.

How can I express my love to my wife? I can take out the trash or help her carry groceries into the kitchen. How can children express love to their parents? They can clean up their rooms or cut the grass.

Love as a feeling is nice, but the feeling means little if it is not put into action.

Putting Love into Action

How can you express love to friends and people around you? And what stops you from doing so more often? Here are three practical steps you can consider as you try to be more loving in your life.

1. Don't Be Afraid to Be Wrong

Rachel was someone who naturally reached out to others. When she was out in public, it was impossible to keep her away from dogs and small children. Loving and reaching out do not come as naturally for most of us as for Rachel. I think part of the reason is that because we have a deep fear of rejection. We are afraid of being misunderstood or of having our love rejected.

We all want to be loved. We all want our affection to be returned when we share it with someone special. There is nothing wrong with that.

But the agape kind of love we have been talking about in this chapter is different. This is a kind of love that seeks the best interest of the other person—not our own interests. This is a kind of love that is more interested in giving than in receiving.

Admittedly, this kind of love may be different from the way you have understood love in the past. My challenge to you is to see that sometimes the deepest and truest form of love is the love that asks for nothing in return.

It is fine for you to want to be loved, and I hope you are loved. Still, it is important that you also seek to love others even when it looks as if you may not be loved in return. I know this can be scary, but there is no reason to be afraid of stepping out and loving other people in a selfless, giving way.

2. Set Boundaries

Some people are afraid that if they reach out to someone to whom no one else reaches out, that person will cling to them. The fear is that suddenly, you'll be "stuck" with a friend who suffocates you.

I think all of us have experienced something like this in life, and that is part of why we don't reach out to certain people. We are afraid of being taken advantage of, so it is safer to leave things the way they are than to risk creating a situation in which we are uncomfortable.

That is understandable, but it also makes sense for those who want to reach out in kindness to be allowed to establish appropriate boundaries. Just because you reach out to someone in love doesn't mean you have to marry this person or concentrate on this person at the expense of your other friends.

Rachel was constantly reaching out in love to people, and I am sure she was often misunderstood. But when misunderstandings arose, she was also quick to say, "I didn't mean it that way." Boundaries are helpful. Just do not make your boundaries so firm and thick that they cannot be penetrated by love.

3. Don't Worry About Your Image

Some young people choose their friends very carefully because they want to protect their image. After all, do you want everyone in the lunch room saying, "Oh my, look at who she's hanging around with now"?

Rachel cared about what other people thought of her. We all do that. But she was different from many people in that she did not let that stop her from reaching out to people in love. She thought loving others was so important that she was willing to risk the damage it might do to her image or the rejection she might suffer from some image-conscious people.

One thing is for sure: if you want to love others, it will be hard work. You will have to think of others instead of always thinking only of yourself. And your image may suffer if you care for people who are labeled as "undesirables." I guess you will just have to decide how important it is to love people, and whether or not your image and personal comfort are more important than showing love.

7
Helping

Rachel based her Code of Ethics on her definition of compassion, which included five key principles: forgiving, loving, helping, leading, and showing mercy for others. One of the most surprising movies of 2000 was an inspiring film called *Pay It Forward*, which is all about the power of Rachel's third principle: helping.

In the movie a young boy named Trevor, played by Haley J. Osment, the young actor who starred in *The Sixth Sense*, started a worldwide chain reaction of goodness by performing a few simple acts of kindness. Eugene Simonet (Kevin Spacey), Trevor's seventh-grade social studies teacher, proposed an interesting project. "Think of an idea to change our world, and put it into action," he told his class.

"The realm of possibility exists in each of you," he said, challenging his students to dream big dreams. "You can do it. You can surprise us. It's up to you."

Some of the students did not know what to make of the

assignment, and some clearly thought Mr. Simonet was nuts. But Trevor took the assignment seriously and developed a plan that he believed could transform the world.

Trevor knew that some people try to "pay back" deeds of kindness that others have done to them by performing good deeds of their own. But he decided to come up with something even more radical: What if instead of paying back good deeds, people paid them forward? In other words, what if people started doing good deeds on their own without waiting for someone else to start the ball rolling?

Trevor developed three simple rules for paying it forward:

1. It has to be something that really helps people.

2. It has to be something they cannot do by themselves.

3. I do it for them, and they do it for three other people.

Some overly cynical film critics dismissed the movie as overly sentimental and unrealistic, but others saw it as a ray of hope in a dark world. An article in *USA Today* even said, "The new movie *Pay It Forward* may be just the ticket for a kindness-starved populace."

The article described how Warner Bros. tried to promote the film by holding special screenings across the United States. A pastor who attended one of the advance screenings was hopeful about the impact it could have.

"I think the human spirit is yearning for meaning, and *Pay It Forward* shows tremendous hope," said Steven Marsh, a Presbyterian minister in Sterling, Kansas, and professor of religion and philosophy at Sterling College. He saw the movie at a special screening with 1,100 Christian, Jewish, and Muslim leaders and college students. "I'm excited about it," he said. "It could inspire people to do some great things."

Apparently, the movie started with a real-life experience of goodness that touched the life of Catherine Ryan Hyde, who wrote the novel on which the movie was based. According to an article in *Time* magazine:

> It all started 23 years ago. A young writer, Catherine Ryan Hyde, was driving home late one night in a disreputable section of Los Angeles when her aging Datsun stalled and started spewing smoke. She leaped out, away from danger, only to see two guys running at her with a blanket. Visions of muggings danced in her head. As she now recalls, "It did not occur to me that this was the good news."
>
> Her car, it turned out, was on fire, burning along the throttle line. It could have exploded and killed her. Instead, some Good Samaritan called the fire department, the two guys with the blanket put out the blaze, and the Datsun was saved to drive another day. It took Hyde a while to understand that she too had been saved. "I finally realized these two guys could have died," she says. "I could have died. I turned around to thank them—and they weren't there. For the next few months, I walked around with this huge sense of regret. But without realizing it, that planted the seed for the idea. If you can't pay it back, pay it forward."

People in Hollywood talked about making the inspirational book into a movie many times. But for filmmaker Mimi Leder, who eventually agreed to direct the movie, it was the encouragement of her thirteen-year-old daughter Hannah that finally changed her mind. "It's our youth who will change the world—

always has been," said Leder. I was of course reminded of Rachel all the way through the movie because it was a powerful presentation of Rachel's chain reaction concept.

One of the more interesting things in the movie is that Trevor was initially discouraged because he couldn't see any immediate positive results from his efforts. He began to doubt that his plan was going to work, even though he had started it fully believing that it would succeed.

What amazed me was that it was working, despite his unbelief, and people didn't really know the effects of what he did until after some bullies tragically killed him at his school.

The end of the movie, which shows a stream of cars and people coming to pay homage to Trevor because he started a chain reaction, particularly moved me. In the same way, Rachel had no idea that her death at Columbine was going to have a similar kind of impact.

You do not have to start a worldwide movement to begin helping people around you. I believe Rachel's life provides many good examples for you to follow.

Fixing a Flat

One of the many people Rachel touched during her life was a young man named Austin Wiggins, who worked as a disk jockey at a Denver radio station. Just like *Pay It Forward* writer Catherine Ryan Hyde, Austin had problems with his car. And the simple way Rachel helped him changed his life.

Austin was driving home one night. He had had a horrible day at work, and then to make matters worse, his car got a flat tire. I don't know if you've ever had a flat tire during the middle of rush-hour traffic, but it can be a horrifying experience. People honk their horns at you for slowing them down, and others give you angry looks or gestures when they pass you.

To make matters worse for Austin, night was coming on, and it began to rain.

Then, out of the darkness, a ray of light emerged. Rachel was driving down the road when she saw a motorist hurriedly trying to pull a spare tire out of his trunk. She pulled up behind him. Then she got out of her car with a flashlight and umbrella and helped him change the flat.

I never heard anything about this incident until after Rachel's death. She would often do things for people, but because for her it was so ordinary, she never really told her family members anything about it. That was the case with Austin.

I first met Austin Wiggins when visiting her gravesite two months after the funeral. I found him watering her grave. Rachel was buried in a new part of a cemetery that, for some reason, didn't have a sprinkler system installed yet.

In the months after the Columbine shootings, Austin put flowers on Rachel's grave. But he also came every single day and watered her grave. Every single day he brought twenty gallons of water and hand watered the parched grass around her grave.

There are thirteen wooden crosses at the head of Rachel's grave representing the twelve students and one brave teacher who were killed at Columbine that day. One of the crosses has Rachel's name on it. Austin wrote a message on that cross saying that through her one act of kindness, she had changed his life forever.

As I talked to Austin at Rachel's grave, he told me how moved he had been that someone had stopped to help him. Then he described how upset he had been, knowing that someone he had met only once in his life had become a victim of the worst school shooting in American history. The whole thing just had a tremendous impact on him. He not only pledged that he would come and water her grave faithfully throughout the summer, but he also vowed that he would spend the rest of his life reaching out through acts of kindness to help others.

Starting Small

Austin Wiggins wasn't the only person I heard from after Rachel's death. For a long time, Rachel had made a point of helping people whenever she could, and as I have said, most of the time she never told anyone about it.

Most of what I learned about her acts of kindness came after her death. I knew that she had done good things for people, but I did not really know the stories. I think that if she looked at what I am writing in this book now or heard the things I talk about when I speak in public, she would be embarrassed by all the attention.

Sometimes she told the people she reached out to her name, while at other times she did not, but in the weeks and months after Columbine we started to receive phone calls and E-mails from people describing the countless small ways Rachel reached out to them and helped them.

I described a number of these cases in *Rachel's Tears*, but one incident not mentioned there stands out to me as particularly significant. A young woman sent an E-mail to tell us about one of Rachel's small acts of kindness.

Apparently, the woman was at a convenience store buying gas and found she was a nickel short. Rachel, who happened to be in the store at the same time, saw the problem, took a nickel out of her pocket, slapped it on the counter, and began to walk out.

When the young woman asked Rachel what her name was, she responded, "Rachel Scott. Glad to be of help, friend."

When the woman realized Rachel had been one of the people killed at Columbine, she was shocked, and she E-mailed us her story. To me, this is a powerful illustration of the fact that help doesn't always have to consist of big things or tremendous acts of sacrifice or bravery. Sometimes, help can be something as small and as simple as giving a nickel to someone who needs one.

Helping others was part of Rachel's lifestyle. It was not something that was accidental or occasional. It was intentional and regular. She never viewed it as a formula. It was just a part of where she had grown, and it was a part of her.

Not Getting Hung Up on Results

Rachel also knew that she could not judge the effectiveness of her deeds by their immediate results, which Trevor struggled with in *Pay It Forward*. For a while, he felt he wasn't making any progress at all—an idea that the ending of the movie proves is woefully misguided. You can never know the full impact of what you do in other people's lives. There are some people who take a while to react or to respond. I know because I am that way sometimes. When I am challenged, I will resist—even if I know it's something I should consider. I know that can be discouraging to people around me.

Rachel realized that she could not tell what was going on inside a person based on what she saw on the outside. She knew that we cannot always judge the end effect of anything we do. Sometimes our acts start a ripple effect that continues far beyond what we could have imagined.

Startling evidence of this truth came to my family when we received the following letter from another person Rachel had helped.

My dear friend Rachel:

You may not remember me but that's okay. For my sanity I pray you do. In case you don't it's me Mark. The guy who moved to Pennsylvania. Anyways I don't know where to start or where to go. I'm sorry. I wish I was there for you, to mourn, to hurt, to cry.

You touched my life Rachel. When you met me I was bitter, and angry at a world that I felt was cruel and unfair to me. But it all changed in 8th. grade. I met several people who help me rise from my state of anger. You were one of them Rachel. You gave me such a positive outlook on life . . . and I never said so much as "thank you."

I am so grateful for meeting you. You inspired me. And for that, I can't begin to thank you enough.

Even though you're in heaven, a place of eternal peace and happiness, we still miss you. I still miss you. To me "you were a person who seemed to care about yourself, but always seemed to care more for others." The strength and courage you showed in living, were nothing short of inspiring. And while it seems hard, we must not live on in sadness but let your courage give us courage, your hope give us hope, and your love give us love.

You know what I once wrote/read:

"Life. For some it's the pursuit of false happiness through money and the acquisition of material possessions. Others find happiness in the pursuit of knowledge, later teaching what they know, leaving their mark whatever way possible. My own journey has been so chaotic that I never really established what life was to me. Until that day. It's all about friends and family. And the smiles; traumas, happiness, and tears shared in each other's pain. To put it simply Rachel, Life is all about love."

And right here and now Rachel, I thank you. You helped to give me life. By simply being my friend . . . I love you for it. While it's hard Rachel, I will go on, we will go on. You're in my thoughts, my heart, and my prayers. And I want you to know one other thing Rachel; you're admired, you're respected, you're missed, and you're loved. By myself and all who were blessed to know you.

Sincerely,
Mark Anthony Farrington Jr.

P. S. Take care and I'll see you someday. That's a promise!!!

Starting from Your Heart

The Bible says that it is more blessed to give than to receive. Most of us have heard that passage, but how many of us believe it? And how many of us put it into practice?

Rachel was someone who heard that passage and responded to it in a powerful way. If you looked carefully at her life, you could see that she was experiencing the truth that helping others ultimately benefits the helper. You may not know it at the time, but when you reach out to others, you become the recipient of things that you cannot really put your finger on, such as true joy and true happiness.

There is fulfillment in giving. The passage that tells us it is more blessed to give than to receive is not just some religious nursery rhyme or fairy tale. It is the truth. We receive more when we give. We experience more life when we give our lives to others. It is an ironic paradox, I know. But it is true.

As I speak around the country and listen to the stories that young people tell me, I am amazed to see what a little kindness can do. In some cities, people are involved in a program called "Random Acts of Kindness" that encourages them to prime the pump and become more conscious of the power of kindness. There are many other solid programs already in existence that pursue similar goals. I will talk about some of them later in this book.

The more I think about such programs, though, the more I believe developing good ways of helping other people ultimately has to be created in each and every person. If helping people merely remains an exterior motivation inspired by one program or another, eventually, it will die.

Reading inspiring stories and hearing the stories of people who have made helping others a part of their lifestyle can make us much more conscious of the many little opportunities that we have to make a difference in someone's life.

I don't go through each day thinking I need to do five acts of kindness today, but when I do see something positive, it challenges me. Sometimes I fail to take advantage of the opportunities that cross my path, and other times I do step out of myself and reach out to someone else. But at least now I'm aware of the need much more than I was before.

Helping others takes time and energy. Sometimes I pass up the opportunity because I am too busy and overcommitted already. I'm supposed to be doing something somewhere, and I feel an urgency to get things done. My priorities become a part of that whole decision-making process.

I am trying to make more time in my live so that I have the time and energy to meet needs when they do arise. I am trying to become a little less frenzied and ragged so that I can respond to the unexpected in life with compassion and grace.

Each one of us is different, and no single program fits us all. But helping others is something we can all do in our own unique ways.

Moving Beyond Fear

Pay It Forward has done more than entertain people. It has inspired them to perform acts of kindness and helpfulness.

After meeting with Catherine Ryan Hyde, the woman who wrote the book that the movie was based on, sixth-graders at Hill Middle School in Novato, California, began helping elderly neighbors with Christmas tree lights, singing carols at convalescent homes, and filming a video to explain the concept of paying it forward. Two inner-city schools in New York City joined together to paint a huge mural depicting their ideas.

Hyde, who helped launch the payitforwardfoundation.com Web site, believes that young people can often be more idealistic and giving than adults. "Grownups have a tendency to talk themselves out of things, saying it will never work, but kids are fabulously optimistic," she says. "I know the book moved some people, and the movie will bring the idea to millions more. Does it have the possibility of starting a social movement? We'll find out."

Why don't more people reach out and help others? I think two of the biggest obstacles are fear and self-protection. People are afraid of what might happen when they reach out, so they focus on safety rather than compassion.

Rachel had an instinctive trust that if she treated people right, they would treat her right. I never knew her to be fearful of people, even from the time she was born. You know how some small children are shy around strangers? Rachel was the opposite. In fact there were times when we had to tell her to be more careful about people she didn't know. She even wrote in her Code of Ethics that perhaps she trusted people too much.

That may be true, but isn't it better to be too trusting than the alternative, a life in which you do not trust others at all, preferring to live a solitary life of bitterness and resentment and fear? I think it's better to reach out than to hide out. We should be cautious, but not fearful or selfish.

Putting Helpfulness into Action

How do you begin to develop a lifestyle of reaching out and lending a hand? Here are three practical steps to get you started.

1. Keep Your Eyes (and Your Heart) Open

The first step in living a lifestyle of helpfulness and kindness is being aware of the needs around us and thinking about how we can respond. None of us can cure the world of all its problems, but each one of us can respond to problems that we see in our daily lives.

There are obvious things. A teacher or a student has an armload of books and is struggling to open a door. The answer is simple: reach out and open the door. These are the kinds of things that we sometimes just ignore, but we all know how grateful we feel when someone reaches out in these ways to us.

Since Rachel's death I've been more conscious of how I can do simple acts that mean a lot. If I am stuck in busy traffic, I can let another driver turn in front of me if he has been waiting there for the last few minutes. I will not let fifteen cars pull out in front of me, but I will let the one guy in, and then maybe somebody behind me will let the next guy in.

This isn't brain surgery, folks, just being conscious of the fact that we are all human beings, and there are times when we each need a break. If you keep your eyes and heart open, you can find many opportunities to provide that break for others.

2. Slow Down

One of the main reasons most of us aren't more helpful is that we are going one hundred miles a minute trying to complete everything we feel we need to get done in our lives. Rachel was a very busy young lady. She had a job at Subway. She was involved in acting in school plays. She was active in her church youth group. But she let everything go whenever someone needed help because she knew that this was a valuable time. What is a ten-minute delay in your life compared to the opportunity to help someone who needs a hand? That was her approach. Many people are too busy, but if we want to be helpful, we will need to take the time.

3. Make It a Priority

We all have many things already competing for time and attention. Some of us even have long "To Do" lists that are already crammed full of more things than we will be able to accomplish in even ten lifetimes.

We will not be successful at developing a lifestyle of helpfulness unless we make being helpful a top priority in our lives. As we'll see, when we do make being helpful a priority, life can be much more fun, exciting, and fulfilling.

8
Leading

Earlier in the book I wrote about the importance of the choices we make because of the inevitable consequences for others and ourselves. Rachel made a decision to be a leader, and leadership was one of her five key principles for starting a chain reaction (forgiving, loving, helping, leading, and showing mercy). As you read this chapter, think about whether you can decide to be a leader when the opportunity presents itself.

"The Tipping Point"

Have you ever wondered how some clothing styles become popular fashion trends, or how certain slogans become everyone's buzzwords? Author Malcolm Gladwell tried to explain the process in his book *The Tipping Point*.

Gladwell argues that any trend or clothing style has a tipping point, which is the point at which enough people are doing "it" to make it into a popular new wave.

For example, why did teen smoking increase 73 percent between 1991 and 1997, which were the same years the Clinton administration spent millions of dollars attacking teen smoking and tobacco companies? Gladwell says that Clinton's anti-smoking campaign, which said, "Smoking isn't cool," was undermined by movies and TV shows and advertising that make it look like smokers *are* cool. For smoking, the tipping point came when enough celebrities and media outlets proclaimed the message that smokers are cool.

Did you ever wonder about Hush Puppies? Maybe you didn't. But ten years ago, these soft, plush shoes were so unpopular that Wolverine, the company that makes them, was thinking about dropping them altogether.

Then something interesting happened. Young urban professionals began going to small, out-of-the-way stores and buying up all the Hush Puppies because they thought they were cool (and nobody else was wearing them). Next, New York fashion designers heard about the yuppies and their Puppies and began featuring the shoes in photo spreads and ads for their new lines of clothing.

Before you knew it, a Hush Puppy craze caught on. In the early '90s, there were only 30,000 pairs of the shoes being sold every year, but in 1995, the company sold 430,000 pairs. In 1996, nearly two million pairs of the shoes were purchased.

I am not bringing all this up because I like the shoes. Rather, I'm trying to make an important point about how trends start and mushroom.

Over the past few years, the media, particularly movies and TV shows, have helped violence become cool. It has mushroomed into an epidemic problem in our society. I do not know whether those who think violence is cool would still think that if a gun or a bomb injured them. Nonetheless, some people just love to see characters being blown away.

This fascination with violence is hurting our society. A change needs to be made, but government officials in Washington cannot stop violence. As with the Clinton administration's anti-smoking campaign, it takes more than money and advertising to change the tide.

School violence and cruelty will stop only if we stop them. In order to do that, we need to start a trend toward compassion and kindness. We need to generate enough momentum to reach a tipping point. If that happens, someday people will think kindness is cool and violence is dumb, better still that kind people are the coolest.

That's what Rachel was trying to do by starting her chain reaction. She believed in the power of influence. She knew that if she threw a stone in a pond, there would be a ripple effect spreading out farther and farther from the center of the pond, just as on the cover of this book.

Rachel believed that she could help start a chain reaction of goodness and love. And if you're reading this book, that shows she's had at least some impact on you.

Looking for Leaders

What do you think of when I use the word *leader*? What kind of picture comes into your head?

I know that some people think that the only people who are true leaders are presidents of countries, or heads of corporations, or maybe conductors setting the tempo for bands or orchestras, or generals commanding large armies, or athletes leading their teams into competition.

There are all kinds of leaders. In fact, I think that just about every one of us is supposed to be a leader from time to time.

Have you ever had a younger brother or sister you had to watch out for? If so, you were a leader to that brother or sister.

Are you planning on ever having children? If so, you will be a leader of your children.

When teachers ask a question in class, have you ever raised your hand and given the answer? If so, you were a leader.

Have you ever been in a group of friends or students who were trying to decide what to do next? If you said, "Hey, I think we ought to do X or Y," then you were a leader.

You may not grow up to be the president of a country or the head of a corporation, but that does not mean you are not a leader. If you have ideas of your own and try to say them out loud or get other people to agree with them, you're a leader.

Part of the reason I am bringing this up is that many people say they feel powerless to do anything to change the world for the better. But if we are going to have a chain reaction of goodness, we will need many leaders who will be willing to stand up and get things going in the right direction.

Will you join me? Will you give your ideas, abilities, and talents to the cause? The following ideas are designed to help you think about ways you can be a leader.

Leaders Are Human

Some people never seem to do anything right. Their lives seem to be a long series of accidents and disasters. I've been reading about one of those people lately. Read this list of personal failures and see if you don't find it depressing:

He was homely and gangly.

He lost his job in 1832.

He was defeated when he ran for the legislature, also in 1832.

He failed in business in 1833.

He lost his sweetheart, who died in 1835.

He suffered a nervous breakdown in 1836.

He was defeated when he ran for speaker of the state legislature
    in 1838.

He failed an attempt for a seat in Congress in 1843.

He lost his bid for re-nomination for Congress in 1848.

He was rejected for the position of land officer in 1849.

He was defeated in a race for the Senate in 1854.

He was defeated for nomination for vice-president in 1856.

He was again defeated for the Senate in 1858.

What a series of miserable mishaps! How could a person who has gone through so much difficulty and failure stand up and try again?

But this person did try again and again. He became president of the United States in 1860, and today he is honored as one of the greatest leaders in world history.

I am of course talking about Abraham Lincoln, an unlikely man who came out of nowhere to lead America at a time when his skills were needed. Lincoln was the country's leader during the Civil War, probably one of the darkest and toughest periods of the nation's history, but he hung in there, and thanks to his unique leadership, the country survived.

You may never be president, but the world needs you to make a unique contribution that only you can make, even if you're only an ordinary person who has gone through a whole series of failures and disappointments.

Leaders Are Servants

One common image of leaders is of a strong, powerful leader over-powering the people he leads. I think of twentieth-century leaders like Adolf Hitler and Joseph Stalin. Hitler led Germany into World War II, causing massive death and destruction. Stalin ruled the USSR with an iron fist from 1924 to 1953, killing millions of his fellow Russians in the process.

Of course, a strong leader doesn't have to do evil things. Perhaps you can think of a recent president you felt did a good job of responding to the needs of the people. There is an important place in this world for gentle leaders.

Once a man named Jesus made an amazing statement. He had noticed that some of His followers were fighting among themselves for positions of power and honor, but He quieted them down when He said: "Whoever wants to become great among you must be your servant." He did more than just say the words. Jesus washed His followers' feet and did many other things to show His servant attitude in action.

When I think of the characteristics that are typical of leaders I admire the most, a servant's heart is at the top of my list. When I say servant, I am not speaking of being a slave. Rather, I am speaking of someone who loves and helps others.

This kind of servant leadership is not necessarily the image we have of leaders like Hitler and Stalin, who were dominating dictators. Maybe we need to think again about what leadership means. Instead of using power to hurt others, the servant leader uses power to help them. Perhaps you can be this kind of servant leader, and instead of causing fear in people's hearts, you will give birth to a chain reaction of kindness and goodness.

Leaders Teach

Many of the leaders I admire also have an ability to communicate their ideas to other people. Rachel did this very well. She wrote wonderful letters to people, and she also put her ideas in poems and songs. Writing helped her get her ideas out of her own head and pass them on to others.

I feel the same way. There are times when I have a strong inner desire to be able to help people understand something. It is a thrill for me to pass on knowledge to others because I am a teacher. That is just part of my makeup. It is exciting for me to pass on things to people, knowing that what I teach just might change their lives forever.

It is a good thing I am a teacher because I have the opportunity to speak to groups of thousands of people around the country. You may never be called on to do that, but you can still pass on what you know and believe to others around you. And you can do that by something I call "imparting."

I believe that some of what we learn comes through instruction, but I believe an even more important element of our education is by impartation, which is the process of learning from someone else by being around him.

We not only learn from listening to what other people say, but we learn by watching their actions and observing their attitudes.

When I was a teenager, there was a man named J. T. Pugh who had a lasting impact on my life. He would speak to large groups of young people about character, morals, and making a difference in the lives of others. He had a peculiar way of tilting his head to one side and occasionally snorting through his nose as he paused between sentences. I was so affected by his demeanor and his message that I would, at times, find myself tilting my head and snorting through my nose as I spoke before a group. As comical as this may sound, I had associated J. T. Pugh's character and nobility with his mannerisms. I wanted so much to be like him that I imitated his actions. This reflects the power of impartation.

Another man who had a powerful impact on my life was Bob Mumford. He was an excellent speaker who could keep an audience enthralled with humor while he got his message across. Bob had a heavy accent, which I would find myself imitating when I would speak before a crowd. I wanted to be like Bob so much that I not only consumed his message, but I also "parroted" his voice and accent.

These are just examples of how leaders have had an impact on my life, but throughout history there have been leaders who were capable of imparting their passion and values to entire nations. Winston Churchill's bulldog approach to World War II and his stirring speech to England were a powerful call to action that imparted strength and resolve to an entire nation. He communicated more than words; he passed on an attitude that resulted in action!

Franklin Roosevelt imparted his fighting spirit to our country through his famous Pearl Harbor "Day of Infamy" speech. Martin Luther King Jr. infused a consciousness into America's soul with his stirring message, "I have a dream." King's message challenged the injustice encountered by the blacks across America and planted seeds of equality for generations to come. His inspiration did not just touch the black community, but convicted and empowered the white community to bring about needed changes.

Rachel never had the chance to speak before large audiences. She would not live long enough to perform on stage or before cameras and impart her talents and message to the world. But that didn't stop her from putting her ideals into action toward the small realm of influence she had at her school. She imparted her code of ethics to a handful of students who will never forget her contribution.

On April 20, 1999, the small, crumpled body of my beautiful daughter lay on the grass outside Columbine High School. Would that be the end of Rachel's dreams to make an impact on the world through acts of kindness? NO, NO, NO! It would only be the beginning! There would be a multitude of young people who would hear her message and pick up the torch that fell from her hands that day. There would be a revolution of kindness that would start a chain reaction far beyond what Rachel could ever have imagined!

Rachel's entire family and I have vowed that her death would not be in vain, but now that cry has gone far beyond us. It has been picked up by multitudes of young people around the world. Her legacy will live on for generations to come. "I dare to believe that I can start a chain reaction through acts of kindness!"

"You Know I Do"

In the days and weeks after Columbine, friends and family of Rachel and the other victims heard differing accounts of their loved ones' final moments. In Rachel's case, only Richard Castaldo knew what had happened before her death. Richard was the young man who was eating lunch with her outside the Columbine library shortly before noon that fateful day.

Understandably, Richard, who was shot more than half a dozen times and remains paralyzed to this day, has problems retrieving memories of that day, but during a January 2000 taping for a segment of NBC's *Dateline* newsmagazine, Richard's mother confirmed that she had heard her son describe Rachel's death in the initial days after the tragedy.

According to Richard's earliest account, he and Rachel were sitting outside when they saw Harris and Klebold approaching. Without warning, the two young men opened fire, severing Richard's spine and shooting Rachel twice in her legs and once in her torso.

As Richard lay stunned and Rachel attempted to crawl to safety, the shooters began to walk away, only to return seconds later. At that point, one of the killers reportedly grabbed Rachel by her hair, held her head up, and asked her, "Do you believe in God?"

"You know I do," replied Rachel.

"Then go be with Him," he responded before shooting her in the head.

In this case, Richard was the only person watching when Rachel reached deep within her soul and decided to remain loyal to her deepest beliefs and values, even though she might have saved her own life if she had been willing to tell a lie. Few people would blame Rachel for trying to find the easy way out of this horrible situation, but she took the hard road, told the truth, and suffered the consequences.

This kind of courage illustrates a powerful lesson about leadership. To be a true leader, you have to be willing to stick to your principles and pay the consequences, no matter what kind of pressure you are under or how many people are watching.

A leader is someone who leads, even if no one is there to see or to follow.

Putting Leadership into Practice

Rachel's code of ethics and her commitment to starting a chain reaction were more than a collection of words or nice ideas. I believe they made up the core of her being, and now her commitment becomes a call to action that challenges young people everywhere to put their beliefs and values into practice.

You may not be a famous or powerful person, but you would be surprised at how you can impart your values and ideas to others around you by living them out with courage and conviction. Lead others not only by your words but also by your actions. By doing so, you will be imparting part of yourself to others.

Maybe you have never thought of yourself as a leader. Maybe you have never even given much thought to leading before reading this brief chapter. Or maybe the things I've said here have caused you to think about being a leader, but now you have not the slightest idea of what to do next.

Below are a few practical suggestions to move you along in the process. If any of these help you to be the type of leader you think you are supposed to be, begin putting them into practice.

Start with Yourself

Some of the young people I talk with seem to have such a lack of self-esteem that they do not believe they can make any difference in someone else's life, not to mention the rest of the world. I can understand how people can be down on themselves, but I also believe that Rachel was right: even small things we can do create a ripple effect that can have a profound effect on the world. You don't have to be a great leader to make a difference. All you have to do is accept the fact that you are worthwhile, that you have a contribution to make, and that you can have an impact on the world around you.

Look Around

I think the next step to growing as a leader is being aware of what's going on around you. Part of that means being aware that your life is meaningful, that you can be helpful to other people, and that what you do and say is going to have an impact on them.

As I said before, this doesn't have to be big things. You don't have to make the game-winning basket in the state championship in order to be a leader. Rather, look to the people and situations nearest you, and think about how you can have a positive impact on them.

It's really the small and simple things that make the biggest impact on most of us. Just think about how you feel when someone pays you a sincere compliment. When someone says to me something like, "You have a kind face," I just melt! Suddenly, that person has penetrated all my defenses and found a soft spot in my heart. This person has found a place of importance in my heart because I feel that he really noticed me or cared for me as a fellow human being. He just started a chain reaction through simple words of kindness. Now I feel better about myself. I am more upbeat and positive. I am in a mood to "prove" that I am what that person said I am, a kind person. So, the ripple effect has started as I reach out to those I meet throughout the day. This was Rachel's secret. She discovered the magic of spreading a few seeds of kindness every day.

Lead Where You Are

Rachel was one of those people who seemed to quickly rise to a leadership position no matter where she was. She was even a leader when she was little and playing with other little kids.

Rachel worked hard to be a leader at church and at school. Leading in her youth group came naturally because Rachel was comfortable organizing things, lining up people to help her, and trying to figure out what kinds of activities could help the group explore the subjects they looked at each week.

At school, she showed leadership not only by reaching out to other students but by giving her all to reach her goals in situations like the class play. Rachel had a servant's heart, but she wanted very desperately to star in the play, and she went after it. The kids competing for the role she wanted say they felt they were at a disadvantage; they didn't have a chance because when Rachel set her mind to something, she got it. And once she got it, everybody agreed that she was perfect for the part of a young girl who dressed and looked different from the rest but had a heart of gold.

You are probably in a number of situations right now in which, if you decided to go for it and really worked hard, you could grow into a positions of leadership that are right for you. Take a look at your life, and think of the areas where you could make a contribution. You might not get a starring role in the class play, but maybe you could build the best sets ever or help create some beautiful background music for the actors.

9
Showing Mercy

I think all of us have probably been in a situation where we have painted ourselves into a corner. We have done something stupid or wrong, and we have been caught red-handed. Or we have been caught in a horrible lie and have had no way to get out of it.

It is a terrible feeling to be caught like this because we know we have messed up. Worse yet, they know that we know they know.

This is a horrible feeling. I know because I have been there. When in that situation, we know we are totally at the mercy of the person who can judge, convict, and sentence us in one move.

I can remember times when instead of condemning me, someone showed mercy to me. Instead of saying, "You are wrong and you will pay," someone said, "You know, I've made some big mistakes myself, and I'm just going to let this mistake of yours go."

This is the essence of mercy, which was the fifth and final key principle that made up Rachel's core values (forgiving, loving, helping, leading, and showing mercy for others).

To Judge or to Show Mercy?

I was in a situation recently where I felt the conflict between judging someone or showing him mercy. It was in a Denver-area courtroom during the trial of a young man who had sold the guns that Eric Harris and Dylan Klebold used to kill the victims at Columbine. A number of the victims' families were there, and I was seated next to my good friends John and Doreen Tomlin, who had lost their son John in the tragedy. We were all there to see that justice was done and that this young man would be punished for his participation in selling the guns.

As I sat there, I remember trying to view this entire situation through the eyes of the one we were there to condemn. Here he was. He had done something wrong. He had illegally purchased guns for minors. And now he was caught, sitting in a courtroom with that deer-in-the-headlights look. I began to think about what would be happening if this young man were being tried for the same situation, but without anyone having been killed. He probably would have received a stern warning and been put on probation, or at worst he would have spent a few days in jail. It was his first offense of any kind. And he certainly never intended for the guns he purchased to be used to kill people.

Unfortunately for him, though, he was in the position of a scapegoat. We could not put the killers on trial because they had killed themselves along with the victims. So he had to face the brunt of our wrath. He became the focal point for justice and punishment. As I was thinking those things, he was asked if he would like to address the courtroom.

As he stood before us with stooped shoulders and sad eyes, he began to softly tell us about how sorry he was that the tragedy at Columbine had happened. He asked for our forgiveness and expressed his guilt at being a part of this terrible situation. He said he never dreamed something like this would happen, and if he possibly could, he would reverse his actions and have no part in the whole thing. He said that he was devastated by the fact that he was involved in any way with our loved ones' deaths.

While I was watching and listening to him, an unwelcome feeling began to express itself in my heart. I began to truly feel sorry for him. I began to think about what Rachel had written about showing mercy to others. I was thinking that if this young man were my son, how would I feel about this whole situation? Yes, I would want him to be accountable for his actions. Yes, I would want him to make some type of retribution with a just sentence. But I would not want him to be the focal point of hatred and unforgiveness, since he was not the murderer. He was not the one who planned this outrageous act. He simply made a huge mistake in purchasing weapons for minors.

I turned to John Tomlin and expressed my struggle, and he admitted that he was feeling the same turmoil within his heart. We both knew that this was not the man who had killed our children, and yet we felt that justice needed to be served. He was sentenced to six years in prison. If Columbine's tragedy were not connected to his part of this violation, he probably would have gotten off much lighter. I am not saying that he shouldn't be punished for his part, but I am saying that I felt a heart of mercy toward this young man, who admitted his wrong and seemed willing to pay for what he had done.

Mercy Reaches Out

There is an old saying that you should not judge another person until you walk a mile in his shoes. That is exactly what we are going to talk about in this chapter.

Earlier we talked about forgiveness, which was another of Rachel's five main methods for starting a positive chain reaction in the world. But as I see it, mercy goes a lot deeper than forgiveness. Forgiveness is wiping the slate clean. It is letting go of the pain and anger that poisons us. It is choosing to not allow bitterness and anger to grow and multiply in our own hearts.

Mercy, I think, goes beyond this. It reaches out to the other person. It extends itself to actually help someone who is in a position where no one else is helping him.

Rachel often showed mercy to people by looking beyond her own issues and needs and focusing on the needs that other people had. It has been said that mercy has feet, while pity is just an attitude. You can pity someone else from a distance, but you have to get close to someone else to show him mercy. And Rachel did this, going out of her way to associate with people who were viewed by others as undesirable.

Rachel was not the only Columbine victim who practiced mercy. Lauren Townsend and Cassie Bernall chose to volunteer in local soup kitchens where they fed and helped needy and homeless people.

To me, this is the essence of mercy. It is saying, "OK, maybe you've really messed up big time here, but I'm not going to condemn you for that. I'm going to reach out to you and pull you up."

Feeling Their Pain

Unfortunately, not everyone feels this kind of mercy being extended to him. There are many people who feel totally isolated from the people around them every day. The Internet allows these solitary souls to send electronic message to others who feel the same way.

In the days after Columbine hundreds of young people did exactly that, according to a *New York Times* article bearing the headline "On-line 'Outcasts' Voice Empathy Toward Killers, Their Alienation."

According to the article, someone with the on-line name "SwimmerK" wrote a message called "A post from an 'outcast,'" which said, "I know how they feel. Parents need to realize that a kid is not overreacting all the time they say that no one accepts them. Also, all of the popular conformists need to learn to accept everyone else. Why do they shun everyone who is different?"

Fourteen-year-old "Mandyjac" replied the next day: "I can't even begin to say all the problems with cliques. I am seen as an 'outcast' and 'dork' by all of the popular people just because of how I act."

As I said above, some people define *mercy* as the attitude that grows when you walk a mile in the other person's shoes. Another word for this feeling is *empathy,* which is the ability to understand or identify with another's feelings or thoughts. Young people around the country clearly could identify with the Columbine killers—perhaps because they had experienced the same kinds of bullying and harassment the killers had endured.

The *New York Times* reporter wrote,

The Internet, which serves as a sounding board for teen-agers' thoughts, offers a glimpse at a . . . painful chord struck by the Colorado killings. In on-line discussions, young people are engaging in what amounts to a fragmented national dialogue over social ostracism and the unforgiving hierarchies of adolescent life, all too familiar but rarely discussed.

Almost all the electronic empathizers were quick to repudiate the killings, but many wrote of identifying with the harassment the two killers, Eric Harris, eighteen, and Dylan Klebold, seventeen, appear to have been subjected to before they acted. At a time when it might be easiest to simply dismiss the two as freaks, several young people seemed to see pieces of their own experience reflected in that of the boys.

The article included a comment from Laura Smith Kay, the on-line editor of *Teen People* magazine, which runs message boards that are featured on America On-line. "They started out mostly saying, 'This is so horrible,' but now they're talking more about cliques and the treatment of outcasts and jocks and how that interaction can create a really unhappy and potentially dangerous atmosphere."

Two additional paragraphs of the article include the reporter's insights into the Internet empathy:

The prevalence of alienation on-line may be partly a result of who uses the Internet. The medium is a refuge for many who consider themselves "outsiders," a place where subcultures of all kinds connect. Harris apparently spent time on-line, maintaining a Web site and playing the computer game Quake, in which the player stalks and kills opponents.

No matter who is typing into the ether, the nature of the on-line dialogue, which provides a sense of anonymity and safety, also provokes the airings of feelings not so easily expressed face to face. In the process, some teen-agers say they find a sense of acceptance on-line they cannot find elsewhere.

Entertainment Overload

Why do some young people feel so cut off from real-life human contact that they retreat into an on-line world to share their thoughts and feelings? This was something Eric Harris and Dylan Klebold routinely did, and over time, they felt so alienated from the flesh-and-blood people around them that they shot them down as coolly as if they were merely characters in a video game.

At a July 2000 meeting of the nation's district attorneys, law enforcement officials discussed the relationship between "virtual realities" and real-world killings.

Retired Army Lt. Col. David Grossman, who spoke at the conference, offered the district attorneys this startling conclusion: "The kids who do this, they develop what I call a bubble. They never experienced real death. They never experienced real suffering. All they've got to go on are TV, movies and video games."

Grossman is the author of a book titled *On Killing: The Psychological Cost of Learning to Kill in War and Society*, which was nominated for a Pulitzer Prize. As he sees it, killers like Eric Harris and Dylan Klebold planned their killings in total isolation from fellow students, and nobody got close enough to them to pop their "virtual bubble."

He thinks that in some cases, media violence helps train alienated young people for real-world acts. He specifically discussed Michael Carneal, the fourteen-year-old boy responsible for the fatal school shooting in Paducah, Kentucky. According to Grossman, Carneal had never shot a real gun until right before he took a neighbor's pistol to school. Instead, he practiced shooting by playing video games.

Grossman isn't alone. Ted Koppel, host of ABC's *Nightline* show, has spoken out about a news and information industry that is "on the verge of becoming a hallucinogenic barrage of images, whose only grammar is pacing, whose principal theme is energy. We are losing our ability to manage ideas; to contemplate, to think." Watergate reporter Carl Bernstein was even more outspoken about the dangers of our new "idiot culture," saying, "For the first time in our history the weird and the stupid and the coarse are becoming our cultural norm, even our cultural ideal."

Hank Hanegraaff, a Christian writer, talks about America's "Technological Tyranny," which threatens to "short-circuit the soul":

> The tragedy at Columbine High is merely one of the latest in a series of wake-up calls. While the prospect of wiring schools for the information age has intoxicated President Clinton, we are losing the souls of our children. Visual stimuli and information bombardment have become a sick substitute for wisdom and understanding. As our kids travel down the information highway, they are picking up a bias against rationality and responsibility.
>
> Lacking the necessary skills to process information, our children have become increasingly nihilistic, and out of that nihilism looms a culture of death.

A Steady Diet of Violence

People have been arguing about media violence for decades. While some people say it is harmful, others disagree, saying it has little to no impact on real-world behaviors.

In July 2000 four of the nation's major health associations issued a statement linking the violence in television, music, video games, and movies to increasing violence among children.

The joint statement by the American Medical Association, the American Academy of Pediatrics, the American Psychological Association, and the American Academy of Child and Adolescent Psychiatry said the effects of media violence are "measurable and long-lasting."

The statement went on to say that "prolonged viewing of media violence can lead to emotional desensitization toward violence in real life. The conclusion of the public health community, based on over 30 years of research, is that viewing entertainment violence can lead to increases in aggressive attitudes, values and behaviors, particularly in children."

We cannot say exactly what caused Eric Harris and Dylan Klebold to do what they did. I do not believe that most people who watch a violent movie are going to go out and kill someone.

But I do believe that repetition eventually shortens the distance between fantasy and reality. Eric and Dylan repeatedly watched *Natural Born Killers*, a violent film about a man and a woman who go on a deadly crime spree. Every time they watched this video once, these two young men took one step closer to Columbine.

All of us are affected by what we watch. We are affected by everything we see, everything we encounter. So if we habitually choose to feed on nothing but violence, we might end up creating violence.

Twenty years ago we didn't have VCRs, so this kind of repetition was impossible outside of movie theaters. When I was in school, there was no way to go home, pop in a video, and watch it over and over again, and it was impossible to pop a game like "Doom" in the console and play it for entertainment hour after hour.

There are good kids who play "Doom," and there are good kids who have watched *Natural Born Killers*. That does not mean they are going to go out and kill someone. But I cannot believe they are not affected by what they see in some way. I think all of us are affected by what we see.

It is the way we are affected that is important. Some of us see a violent movie and are disgusted, while someone else will see the same movie and say, "Wow! That's cool how they blew that guy's head off." Eric and Dylan fed on violence so regularly and so repetitiously that the line between fantasy and reality grew thinner and thinner until it disappeared.

Some people are much more susceptible to violence in media than others, so maybe 999,999 people out of a million can watch *Natural Born Killers* with no danger of them going out and killing someone, but the one person who is susceptible is at a much greater risk.

Others Are at Fault Too

It would be silly to lay all the blame on violent media. Rather, I would argue that at least part of the problem lies with parents and "friends" who never got close enough to these two troubled young men to puncture their self-created bubble and reach out to them with a powerful display of love and mercy.

Eric actually said on one of the videotapes he and Dylan made before the shootings that he didn't want to get too close to his parents because he didn't want to be bonded with anybody who might know what they were doing.

In a sense, I really think Rachel was trying to reach out to Eric and Dylan and help them. When she confronted them about the videos, she was trying to help them, not to judge them or hurt them. She recognized trouble. She recognized something was wrong. And she loved them enough to be willing to put herself in a position of rejection. Her confrontation was a form of merciful helping.

There are times in life when we should show mercy, and other times when we must call for accountability. We have to know where those boundaries are.

We must never inflict torment on someone simply for the purpose of inflicting torment. We should not ever hurt someone simply to hurt him. Sometimes we will be forced to hurt people to help them. For example, we pay for doctors to hurt us to get rid of a bigger hurt. We pay dentists huge amounts of money to drill our teeth and make holes in them and put foreign objects in them and pull them, all of which is torture. But we know that the pain is for our own good.

Likewise, there are times when we must reach out in mercy and pierce another person's bubble—whether that is a "virtual reality" bubble, or a media violence bubble, or merely a bubble of self-imposed alienation and hatred.

Piercing that bubble may hurt the other person, but if it is done with mercy and love, it can be a tool that is used to help and heal him.

Being a "See-Througher," Not a "Look-Atter"

Years ago I learned an incredible lesson from a wise old man by the name of Norman Grubb. Norman was born in England, and his family was close to the royal family. His brother served as one of Winston Churchill's right-hand men during World War II. Norman had been friends with several presidents and had written numerous best-selling books during the 1950s. Despite all of his accolades, he was one of the most honest and humble men I have ever known.

He stayed in my home numerous times when I was in my twenties and early thirties. I'll never forget a simple lesson he taught me as we were having a discussion one day. He said, "Darrell, we live in a world of illusions. If you want to really be fulfilled in life, you must learn to see through the illusions to the reality. If you will learn to be a 'see-througher' instead of a 'look-atter,' life will have far more meaning." That simple statement from Norman Grubb was to change my life forever.

Most of the time, people look at circumstances instead of seeing through them. We focus on the superficial surface instead of see-ing the deeper reality. We judge others so easily by viewing their clothes, facial expressions, body language, and so forth instead of taking a caring look at their hearts. Mercy triumphs over judgment when we learn to be a "see-througher."

Rachel always had an inquiring mind. She longed for more than superficial answers, and sometimes her persistence could even be annoying. I'll never forget the time that she and her sisters, Bethanee and Dana, asked me, "Dad, why is the moon following the car?" Being a teacher by nature, I launched into a scientific explanation about everything from the gravitational pull of the moon on the tides to Einstein's theory of relativity, when I sud-denly looked at my three little girls and started laughing at the strange expressions on their faces. Finally, one of them said, "Dad, what are you talking about?" They then repeated the question, "Why does the moon follow the car?" At that point I was so exas-perated that I simply said, "Because it wants to," which seemed to satisfy them completely.

Rachel, though, would often ask penetrating questions. The older she got, the less satisfied she was with pat answers. She would always dig a little deeper. Several times my discussions with her caused me to go and do some digging of my own. In the last few years before her death, her hunger to understand the myster-ies of life only grew more intense. During these years, she asked questions like "Why is there so much evil in our world?" Over the years we had some pretty deep discussions about some of these questions. When I saw her journals after her death, I was filled with tremendous joy because I saw reflected in her written words many of the things we had talked about.

I remember one time she asked me to explain why the sun rose in the morning and why it set at night. I tried to explain that the idea of the sun setting and rising was really just an illusion. I told Rachel that the sun never really rose or set, but that it just kept shining brightly all day long. From our perspective on earth, it looked like the sun was rising and setting as we circled around it. But that was just our perspective, and the truth was bigger than what we could see.

This led into a rather deep discussion about how we live in a world of illusion, and many things are not the way they seem. We had a lengthy discussion about the difference between eternal things and transitory things, true things and false things; we talked about how the things we see are not to be trusted, but the things that are invisible are more real.

Some time later, Rachel wrote about sunrise and sunset in her journal. In addition, there was a girl named Lindsay who had a class with Rachel two years before Rachel died. Lindsay said Rachel talked to her one day about the difference between real things and illusory things, and it was something that stuck in Lindsay's mind. "She made me think," Lindsay told me one day. "She planted seeds in my own thinking that have never gone away."

In one of her journals Rachel used the metaphor of a camera to express her feelings about the visible world of matter and the invisible world of spirit. She concluded that her true essence could not be captured on film.

I loved Rachel's hunger to plumb the depths of a thing, and I think her journals demonstrate the fact that she was never content with just a superficial kind of understanding or existence. She wanted to go deeper into the reality of the cosmos and bypass those things that were transitory or illusory.

This is the essence of what it means to be a see-througher, not a look-atter.

Pictures
Pictures of my life
Everything captured
   on endless black and white film
Every moment, every angle, everyone
   Where I am both the
      photographer and the poser.
Every sorrow, every laugh
Every kiss, every hurt
Censored to the public
      Seen by my soul mates
Captured by my hand
Posed by my naked soul
No... by my naked body
For even the film
      cannot capture my true form
   My true existance

Another example of the difference between being a look-atter and a see-througher is in the world of science. Science tells us that everything we call solid matter is really pulsing energy. You may think this book you're holding is a solid thing full of solid pages of paper, but everything we can see, touch, and hold is nothing more than energy in constant motion. Our senses tell us one thing, and the facts tell us another, so we are forced to believe the illusion or believe the facts. Even though it doesn't always make sense to me, I believe the facts. Faith is simply believing the facts instead of the illusion.

Seeing Differently Can Lead to Mercy

Seeing through as opposed to looking at makes it easier to show mercy. Instead of looking at the outward surface of what people are doing and judging them, we can see through their actions to their hearts and show them mercy. I believe that if more of us did that, there would be fewer Columbines.

John Nicoletti is a psychologist who wrote a book about Columbine and consults with law enforcement agencies about teen killers. He says that school killers put out signals before they kill, and that it is up to people who are around them to read the signals.

In the months before the killings, Eric and Dylan made videotapes full of violent rantings, created a Web site full of their views, and wrote a death-filled essay for one of their Columbine classes. Nicoletti told the Colorado Governor's Columbine Review Commission that such activities are trial runs.

"Practice sessions involve pushing the edge of the envelope," he said. "They may not be real extreme to start with; that's why they get away with them."

An FBI agent who also spoke to the commission agreed. "People do not simply wake up in the morning and decide to be violent," said the agent. "There are signs along the way. They may be subtle signs, but there are signs."

I challenge you to be the kind of person who can see through outward appearances and recognize the signs and signals people around you are sending out. If you do that, you're on your way to showing people mercy.

Putting Mercy into Practice

We've been talking about showing mercy in this chapter. This may be a relatively new concept for you to grasp. If so, here are practical suggestions about how you can begin showing mercy to others around you.

Remember Your Crises

At the beginning of the chapter, I talked about cases where I was caught red-handed doing something wrong, but instead of others judging and punishing me, they showed me mercy.

Has this ever happened to you? If so, remember the ways in which mercy was shown to you, and use that as an example for showing it to others. The Bible says, "Blessed are the merciful, for they shall obtain mercy." Perhaps if you show mercy to others, you will experience more of it.

Get the Whole Story

Instead of watching the world from a distance and passing judgment on what another person does, go to that person, and get his side of the story. I talked earlier about the young man who sold the guns to Eric and Dylan. I was able to hear his side of the story, and I believed that he never meant for students to be killed at Columbine.

Perhaps you could make similar efforts to find out why people do what they do instead of merely passing judgment on them for doing it. Rachel would often do this. When something happened that she didn't understand, she would walk right up to someone and find out what was going on. In the case of Eric and Dylan and their violent videos, the more she knew, the more upset she was. But she still cared for the two lost boys who were making these destructive videos.

If someone hurts you, try responding in this way. Instead of going and telling five of your friends what the other person did, go to that person and say, "John, I just want to confirm something and find out if it's true. Did you say this? And did you mean it to be hurtful?" You may be surprised to get more information that changes your perception.

Knowing the whole story will help us to show mercy if it is

appropriate. Sometimes accountability is the more appropriate concern. If I see someone with a knife dripping with blood and I find someone stabbed to death in the next room, it is time to call the police. When that killer has been held accountable and given appropriate consequences, mercy can have its time and place.

Developing Your Own Code of Ethics

In this section of the book, we've focused on exploring Rachel's five key principles: forgiving, loving, helping, leading, and showing mercy for others.

I believe these are solid principles, but now it's time for you to develop your own code of ethics. As I have said, your code has to be something that belongs to you. It has to reflect your unique concerns, abilities, and sensitivities.

There is no single list of principles to live by. Over the centuries, many people have developed codes of ethics that were right. Perhaps some of the conclusions they have reached can help you come up with your own code of ethics. Let the following statements inspire you and guide you as you seek to find ways to reach out to others with caring and compassion:

- Albert Einstein: "Only a life lived for others is worth living."
- Whoopi Goldberg: "When you are kind to someone in trouble, you hope they'll remember and be kind to someone else. And it'll become like a wildfire."
- Martin Luther King Jr.: "Life's most persistent and urgent question is, 'What are you doing for others?'"
- Eleanor Roosevelt: "When you cease to make a contribution you begin to die."

- The Talmud: "A person who seeks help for a friend while needy himself, will be answered first."

- Mother Teresa: "We realize that what we are accomplishing is a drop in the ocean, but if this drop were not in the ocean, it would be missed."

- Marcus Aurelius: "Waste no more time talking about great souls and how they should be. Become one yourself!"

- Cicero: "It is our special duty, that if anyone needs our help, we should give him such help to the utmost of our power."

- Gandhi: "Be the change you want to see in the world."

- Goethe: "Kindness is the golden chain by which society is bound together."

- Ruth Smeltzer: "You have not lived a perfect day, even though you have earned your money, unless you have done something for someone who will never be able to repay you."

- Katharine Hepburn: "Love has nothing to do with what you are expecting to get—only what you are expecting to give."

- John Watson: "Be kind—everyone you meet is fighting a hard battle."

- Abraham Heschel: "When I was young, I admired clever people. Now that I am old, I admire kind people."

As you can see, there are many ways to start a chain reaction. In the following chapters we will be looking at even more specific ways to make that happen.

10
Identifying the Needy in Our Midst

I wish that I had never been put in the position to write this book. I wish that my life had gone on its normal course, and that Rachel and the other twelve victims of the Columbine tragedy had been able to live long and productive lives.

But that was not the way things turned out. Their lives were cut short, and my life—along with the lives of other family members and friends—was instantly turned upside down.

Even sadder is the fact that Columbine was not the first school shooting, and it probably will not be the last, no matter how many new laws we pass or how many security guards and metal detectors we install in our schools.

Our society includes many lost and fragile souls who find their lives sinking out of control and decide to take others down with them. The record of recent school shootings is a sorrowful one:

- Fort Gibson, Oklahoma, December 6, 1999. A thirteen-year-old student fires at least fifteen rounds at Fort Gibson Middle School, wounding four classmates. Asked why he did it, he replies, "I don't know."

- Deming, New Mexico, November 19, 1999. Twelve-year-old fellow student shoots a thirteen-year-old girl in the head. She dies the next day.

- Conyers, Georgia, May 20, 1999. A fifteen-year-old boy opens fired at Heritage High School with a .357-caliber handgun and a rifle, wounding six students.

- Springfield, Oregon, May 21, 1998. A teenage boy opens fire at a high school after first killing his parents at home. Two teenagers are killed, and more than twenty people are injured.

- Fayetteville, Tennessee, May 19, 1998. Three days before graduation, an eighteen-year-old honor student opens fire at a high school, killing a classmate who was dating his ex-girlfriend.

- Edinboro, Pennsylvania, April 24, 1998. A science teacher is killed in front of students at an eighth-grade dance by a fifteen-year-old shooter.

- Jonesboro, Arkansas, March 24, 1998. Four girls and a teacher are killed and ten people are wounded at a middle school when two boys, eleven and thirteen, fire from nearby woods.

- West Paducah, Kentucky, December 1, 1997. Three students are killed and five others wounded when a fourteen-year-old student opens fire at Heath High School.

- Pearl, Mississippi, October 1, 1997. A sixteen-year-old boy kills his mother, then goes to his high school where he shoots nine students, two fatally.

- Bethel, Alaska, February 19, 1997. A sixteen-year-old boy takes a shotgun and a bag of shells to school, where he kills the principal and a student and injures two others.

After each of these ten horrible episodes, people all over the country scratched their heads and searched their souls wondering how troubled boys could inflict so much pain and suffering on others. Meanwhile, law enforcement officials and school administrators intensified their efforts to develop ways to identify potential killers before they struck out.

But long before school shootings gained worldwide attention and headlines, Rachel was engaged in her own program of identifying and reaching out to the most needy people around her.

I believe that if more of us followed her approach, there would be far fewer Columbines, Jonesboros, and West Paducahs erupting into violence and death. In addition, lost souls would feel less angry and alienated, and our schools—even our entire society—would be happier and healthier.

Having a Plan

Doing good is not something you can do indiscriminately if you hope to have any real impact on the world. In fact, starting a chain reaction is like anything else you're trying to do: it helps to have a plan.

One reason good people need to be more intentional about their work is that people who are trying to disrupt the world and cause havoc for others often have well-thought-out plans to guide their work.

At least that was the case for Eric Harris and Dylan Klebold, according to *Denver Post* writer Trent Seibert. He writes in his article

"Columbine Killers Claim from Grave to Be Rebels with Cause" that the two teens extensively planned their attack, which they hoped would "kick start a revolution."

In videotapes they made before the attack, Harris and Klebold promised to haunt the survivors from beyond the grave and half jokingly debated whether Steven Spielberg or Quentin Tarantino would film their life stories.

According to the article, Harris said the attack was designed to express anger toward his military family that often moved, saying he had to start over "at the bottom of the ladder." Klebold wanted to harm his popular, athletic brother, Byron, and Byron's friends who repeatedly "ripped" on him.

"As far back as the Foothills Day Care center, Klebold hated the 'stuck-up' kids who he felt hated him, 'I'm going to kill you all,' he said. 'You've been giving us [expletive] for years.'"

The two teens did express regrets for the trouble they would inflict on their parents. "It [expletive] sucks to do this to them," Harris said. But Harris also said he believed he knew what his parents would say after the killings: "If only we would have searched their room. If only we would have asked the right questions."

Harris also seemed to fear that after school shootings in Oregon and Kentucky, he and Klebold would be seen as copycats. "Do not think we're trying to copy anyone," he said, mocking the Kentucky shooters. The Columbine attack plan was better, he said, "not like those [expletive] in Kentucky with camouflage and .22s. Those kids were only trying to be accepted by others."

Rachel Targeted Students Too

As I listened to some of these horrifying tapes, it became clear to me that their rampage was not random. Eric and Dylan had targeted their high-caliber rage against jocks, blacks, and Christians.

Likewise, as I began reading Rachel's journals after her death, I saw that she, too, had targeted students at school. But whereas Eric and Dylan planned to kill their targets, Rachel only wanted to love hers.

Rachel came to the conclusion that there were three major groups in her school that were feeling left out, and these became her targets for acts of kindness. I'm not sure that she actually sat down and said, "I'm going to perform six acts of kindness toward members of these three groups today." It wasn't that clinical. But it was intentional, and it was based on the needs she saw around her every day in the classrooms and hallways of Columbine.

The three groups Rachel reached out to the most were the kids who were disabled, those who were new at school, and those who were picked on by others.

I don't know exactly how she came to focus on these three groups, but she did. Perhaps these were the groups whose pain she was most aware of. Perhaps she saw repeated incidents of these kids being harassed at school, and instead of turning away she turned toward them in compassion and love.

Your school or situation may be completely different from Rachel's, and it may be different types of people whose pain reaches out and grabs your heart. Still, I think it might be helpful for you to learn about how Rachel targeted specific people for compassion and kindness. Perhaps her example can help you see how you can reach out to specific kinds of people who especially need affection and recognition.

Adam's Story

I never know when someone is going to walk up to me and tell me another story about how Rachel had reached out to him in the midst of his need.

In the summer of 1999 I was at Coors Field in downtown Denver for a benefit softball tournament organized to help the Columbine families and the community. More than twenty-three thousand people turned out for the benefit, which featured members of the Denver Broncos, the Colorado Avalanche, the Colorado Rockies, and the Denver Nuggets who had given up their free time to help heal a community that had been wounded by the worst school shooting in American history.

My son Craig threw out the opening pitch to get the whole thing started, and as I was watching the game unfold, a young man named Adam approached me and told me his story.

Adam attended Columbine, but he wasn't like all the other students. He had been born with several disabilities. As a result, he talked very slowly, he looked much older than his age, and his facial muscles drooped, causing him to look different from all the others. As a result, he was picked on and intimidated at school. Adam told me that he was routinely made fun of because of his appearance. Kids at school called him "alien" and other hurtful names.

Adam told me that Rachel treated him differently from the way all the other kids did. She always had a kind word for him as she saw him in the hallway or in the cafeteria. Over time, these gestures of kindness became the highlights of every day, and Adam began to look forward to them as he prepared to go to school.

The morning of April 20, 1999, Rachel saw Adam in the hallway and smiled at him. Then she came up to him and said, "Adam, we're going to have lunch together next week, just you and I, and nobody else. And I want you to tell me all about your family." They agreed to meet the following week, and as Rachel got ready to head off to class, she said, "Adam, I just want to be your friend."

But then, suddenly, Rachel was gone.

Adam began crying as he told me his story. Then I broke down and started crying with him. It was just one of those times that you feel all torn up inside and have to reach out and hug someone, so I reached to Adam and gave him a hug.

As I was holding this young man in my arms, something welled up inside of me, and I made a vow before God and before Adam that, with his permission, I would share his story with other kids as I spoke around the country. Adam said OK.

Since then, I have probably shared his story with close to a million young people. Many more will read the story in this book. My hope and prayer are that you will do more than say, "My, isn't that a nice story?" I hope and pray that you look for Adams in your midst and reach out to them as Rachel did to him.

"Welcome to Columbine, Friend"

Some of the stories I heard about the things Rachel did came from young people who E-mailed us after she died. One of these people was a girl named Amber Jackson.

According to Amber, every time Rachel went into the Columbine cafeteria, she would look around for new faces. When she spotted someone who looked as if he might be new at school, she would walk over and say, "Hi, I'm Rachel Scott. Are you new at school?"

We have all been the new kid at school or somewhere during our lives. At a big school like Columbine, which has more than 1,600 students, every new kid wants somebody to reach out to him. Rachel did that, and she made a lot of friends in the process.

About a week before the shootings at Columbine, Amber moved

to Georgia. When she heard about Rachel's death, she E-mailed us with her story.

Amber's mother had been killed in an auto accident, and Amber moved to Colorado to attend Columbine. On her first day at the school, she was feeling lonely and sorry for herself, so she sat down in the corner of the cafeteria all by herself. But the next thing she knew, Rachel walked up to her with a big smile, introduced herself, and asked Amber if she was new at school.

Amber said yes, so Rachel gathered up a bunch of her friends to come and have lunch with Amber.

I talked to Amber after reading her E-mail, and she said that because of Rachel's kindness, what would have been the worst day of her life at a school became instead one of the best days of her life.

When news of the Columbine tragedy broke, Amber was at her new school in Georgia. She said all she could think about was the young girl who had made such an impact on her life with such a simple but profound act of kindness.

Helping Those Who Are Picked On

Every day in schools across America, thousands and thousands of young people feel as if they are being picked on. Is this any different from when I was in school many, many years ago? I am not sure it is.

I know we have bigger schools now where hundreds and possibly thousands of kids are crammed together every day for nearly eight hours. And size does make a difference.

But some things haven't changed at all. For as long as there have been kids, the young years have been the most vulnerable years. Kids are growing up. Their bodies are changing, and inside, hormones are raging. Young people are finding their own identities, carving out their own personalities and seeing how these differ from those of their parents or their friends.

All of this change brings about feelings of insecurity, and bullying is one of the results of that insecurity. Sometimes those who feel bad about themselves feel better when making life miserable for others.

There have always been bullies in schools. I can remember instances in school that have scarred me for life. I can still recall feelings of fear, anger, and tremendous anxiety from my high school days. Frankly, there were days when I felt like staying in bed because I didn't think I could face going to school.

The terrible thing is that high school could be the most wonderful experience if it weren't full of so much nastiness caused by bullies abusing other people to boost their own fragile egos. The school could be a haven where everyone is a friend, but for too many people school is a place of turmoil and torment. That is because not enough people are doing enough good to influence things in the right direction.

Efforts to Reach Out

Rachel knew she wasn't perfect, and she had her own share of doubts and insecurities, but somehow she was able to look beyond her own problems and focus on the needs of kids who were really being picked on and bullied.

Rachel reached out in this way to Dylan Klebold, who responded to her care by developing a crush on her. Today, many people see Dylan as little more than someone who represents everything that is wrong with young people today, but prior to the shootings he helped orchestrate, he was another student who simply fell through the cracks at Columbine.

According to the folks who knew him best, seventeen-year-old Dylan Klebold was pretty much like most other high school kids, only nicer.

A friendly kid who was born into a loving, affluent home and who joined the Boy Scouts and played Little League during his younger years, Klebold had attended Columbine's prom three nights before the shooting, telling his friends that he hoped they wouldn't lose touch with each other when they all went off to college that fall.

There were subtle signs that not everything was as placid as it seemed. Klebold, whose mother was Jewish, sometimes surprised his bowling buddies when, after rolling a ball down the lane, he would say, "Heil, Hitler!" They thought he was joking.

Klebold and his friend Eric Harris did have a run-in with the law after they were caught burglarizing a van. And Klebold was a part of a Columbine group who wore long coats and called themselves the Trench Coat Mafia. Still, no one who knew him suspected Klebold could ever be involved in something as horrible as the Columbine killings.

Most of the time, Dylan channeled his creative energies into audio and video production. In fact, it was Dylan who helped run the sound at a school talent show Rachel performed in before she died.

Still, this young man felt so alone and alienated that he teamed up with Eric Harris to eliminate all his perceived enemies. I find it amazing to consider the amount of anger and rage that must have built up to cause someone to do that.

Since Rachel's death, I have heard many stories about how she reached out to Eric and Dylan. I don't know any details, but some of her friends told me that she confronted them about some of the violent videos they were making. I wish I knew what she had said, but I probably never will. But at least I know she intentionally reached out to these two troubled young men—both out of compassion and out of concern.

Watching Out for Warning Signs

Columbine helped turn the attention of researchers and law enforcement people all over the country to the problem of school violence. Among those researching the problems was the Federal Bureau of Investigation, which developed a list of telltale traits held in common by many of the young men who had been behind the school shootings listed at the beginning of this chapter.

Washington Post reporter David A. Vise summarized some of the FBI's key traits:

Personality Traits and Behavior

- intentional or unintentional clues to feelings, thoughts, fantasies, or attitudes that may lead to a violent act
- low tolerance for frustration
- poor coping skills
- inability to bounce back from a frustrating or disappointing experience
- failed love relationship
- resentment over real or perceived injustices
- depression
- narcissism
- alienation
- intolerance
- inappropriate humor

- lack of trust
- negative role models such as Hitler or Satan
- associates with a single group of people
- unusual interest in sensational violence
- fascination with violence-filled entertainment
- drawn to inappropriate role models associated with violence and destruction

Family Dynamics

- turbulent parent-child relationship
- parents' refusal to recognize or acknowledge problems in their children
- access to weapons
- family lacks closeness
- parents give in to child's demands
- no limits or monitoring of television and Internet

School Dynamics

- student is detached from school, students, and teachers
- tolerance for disrespectful behavior
- behavior that is unyielding and insensitive toward others
- treats some students better than others
- code of silence
- unsupervised computer access

Social Dynamics

- student is part of peer group that is fascinated with violent or extremist beliefs
- use of drugs and alcohol

Although the FBI admits that there's no guaranteed way to find out who the next school shooter will be, school officials all over the country have used these traits to look out for students who might be in trouble.

There is another way this list can be put to use. Concerned and caring students might study this list of traits in order to identify kids who need a kind word, a smile, or a helping hand. I believe that everyone would rather be loved than hated, and that everyone would rather love than hate, and the FBI's research may help lead us to the kinds of people who need these gestures of affection most of all.

An Author's Silent Pain

Frank Peretti is a best-selling writer whose fast-paced novels explore the challenges of people who find themselves in the middle of battles between good and evil.

But when he hasn't been sitting at a computer keyboard, Peretti has been thinking about some of his childhood traumas. In a recent interview with *Publishers Weekly,* Peretti described how his own battles with a childhood deformity called cystic hygroma inspired his latest book, a memoir titled *The Wounded Spirit:*

> Psychologically, as long as I was home with my family, I coped just fine. But when I went to school and started meeting other kids, that was a different animal. That was when I realized that something was wrong with me, and I became very introverted. It didn't help that I was also very small—a small, frail freak.

Peretti says his sense of alienation intensified his interest in monsters and the reality of evil.

Back then I had a definite obsession with whatever was evil and ugly and scary. Because I was so introverted, I spent a lot of time in my room creating scenarios with that stuff. I suppose I still have a little bit of that ability to create a scary situation or character.

According to Peretti, his deep religious values prevented him from becoming someone who would act out his pain and frustrations on others.

Because of my Christian faith, I had a strong moral foundation and a sense of right and wrong. My parents raised me to turn the other cheek and not inflict wounds. But my sophomore year in high school, I came to the end of my rope. What changed it all for me was that a gym teacher—the last person on earth I thought would care—asked me if I was okay. I'd never had anybody ask me that at school before. And so I wrote a letter. I was afraid to talk to him face to face, but I knew I could write.

Ultimately, it was the horrors of Columbine that persuaded Peretti to take a break from his popular fictional books and write *The Wounded Spirit,* a nonfiction book.

Last year I was asked to speak in Ontario, California, just one month after the Columbine massacre. As I thought about it, it was no wonder to me that [Eric] Harris and [Dylan] Klebold took their bombs and guns to school, since school was the source of their pain. There's plenty of testimony from the other students that these kids were outcasts. They were called faggots; they were squirted with ketchup. Among all of the other influences that may have caused their violent spree—the video games, the music, etc.—no one was talking about this basic thing. So that's what I spoke about at the event.

Peretti's comments show that it is common for young people to face personal problems and deal with difficult feelings of loneliness and alienation. Less common are people who are willing to reach out to troubled kids with compassion and kindness.

Will you be one of these people?

Identifying and Reaching Out to the Needy

People have all kinds of problems and needs. No one can respond to them all, but perhaps you can respond to some of the people and problems you see around you on a daily basis.

If you are interested in trying to reach out, here are some practical suggestions to get you started.

Turn On Your Radar and Get Involved

It does not take superhuman ability to feel the pain of others. All it takes is a bit of sensitivity and perhaps an intentional effort to turn on your radar.

Most young people have eaten in a school lunchroom enough times to be able to spot a new face. It is easy to take a quick look around the lunchroom and see if there is someone you have never seen before. If you see someone who looks out of place, walk over and say hello. Is that a lot to risk?

Simply look around, and when you see someone new, walk up to him and say, "I don't think I've ever met you. Are you new at school?" And if he says yes, welcome him to your school. It does not mean you have to be best friends with him; it just means that you are reaching out and helping him connect in a new and frightening environment.

It is also easy to notice when people are being picked on. Now there may be situations when getting personally involved might put you at risk of becoming the bully's next victim. Maybe it would be better to find a teacher or a school official and let him know what's going on. You might be labeled a tattletale, but I would prefer that to watching someone getting the tar beaten out of him. Later on, when things cool down, you can talk to the victim and reach out on a personal level.

As I've said, no amount of rules or security guards is going to stop school violence. As long as there are angry people, there will be bullying, intimidation, and violence. But you can help stop these things and turn the tide, making our schools better places for everyone.

Instead of being silent or walking away, step up to the plate and get involved. That person who is being picked on is in tremendous torment and will appreciate your help.

Move Toward "Oddballs" Instead of Running Away from Them

I saw the movie *The Elephant Man* years ago, but it has really stuck with me. It was about a badly deformed man named John Merrick who was ridiculed for his hideous appearance. But Merrick was befriended, and soon people saw that inside his ugly exterior Merrick was a beautiful soul.

Rachel was a person who could look beyond people's appearances and reach out to the person and the soul deep inside. She simply saw that some people were hurting, and it was her instinct to reach out and help them.

Maybe in the case of people like Eric Harris and Dylan Klebold, the pain and alienation were already so strong that no one was going to be able to reach them. I think that kind of situation is extremely rare. Most people want others to show signs of friendship. All it takes is someone who is willing to move in their direction.

Give Up Your Lunch Hour

School can be tough. You have to get up early in the morning and get dressed. Then you have to spend hour after hour in classes with people you may not really want to be with. But then comes lunchtime, and for a half hour or so you are suddenly free to do more of what you want with whomever you want.

Rachel saw the lunch hour as her chance to reach out to people who needed her kindness. Rachel was comfortable with herself and had a lot of friends in every class, but she was motivated by something deeper. She got fulfillment from knowing that she was making somebody else feel welcome.

You don't have to give up all your lunch hours, but perhaps you could keep your eyes and heart open to people who may be sitting all by themselves among hundreds of other students who are talking and laughing together. For Rachel this wasn't a huge sacrifice. It was something she enjoyed doing. Maybe you could learn to enjoy it too.

11
Welcoming the Outcasts

We've talked about the ways Rachel identified some of the lonely and needy people in her midst, and I have shown a few ways you can reach out too. But there is another step you must take if you are to truly cause a positive chain reaction that expands outward in all directions, and that step involves extending a welcome to the outcasts in your midst.

You have probably seen big "Welcome" signs at stores, or houses that have a "Welcome" mat by the front door. These are designed to show people that they can come on in and that they will be greeted and accepted when they do.

But it's one thing to hang up a "Welcome" sign and quite another to develop a welcoming heart that is open to people who need warmth and encouragement. Rachel had that kind of heart, and she wrote about it in a short story she titled "Gloves of Conviction."

I don't think she wrote it for a class at school. I don't even think she wrote it for anybody else to read. Rather, it was something she wrote out of her heart after failing to care for somebody as she felt she should have.

The story is about a needy-looking woman who came into the Subway sandwich shop where Rachel worked. I think we have all been in similar situations, and typically, many of us prefer to turn away and mind our own business rather than reach out to someone who obviously looks as if she could use our help.

For Rachel, this one episode of failing to help someone who was more vulnerable than she was troubled her deeply and inspired her to write this story. I hope this story helps you understand a little bit better what a welcoming heart looks and feels like.

Gloves of Conviction

I was opening that day for work. On Sundays, no other employees come in until 11:00, which meant I had two hours of work to do by myself and then open the store for another hour alone with customers.

Usually no one comes in until about 11:30 on a Sunday morning anyway, so I always have plenty of time on my hands. I couldn't believe how windy and cloudy it was. The cold of the breeze alone could bring you to a chill.

It was 10:00 so I flipped the switch for the open sign and unlocked the doors. It must have only been five minutes after that when I heard the doorbell ringing, telling me I had a customer. I went out front and began to put the gloves on, ready to make the first sandwich of the day.

I looked up and saw a woman who must have been in her late forties. She was wearing several layers of clothes. They were torn and dirty. Her face was dark from dirt. She was shivering, and then she began to cough in an almost uncontrollable manner. She looked up at me after she was all right and she gave me such a warm smile.

"What can I do for you, Ma'am?" I asked.

She looked at me pleasantly and said, "Oh, I was just wondering if you happen to know what time the busses were coming. I have been waiting out in the cold for two hours. You think they wouldn't be so late, especially on a Saturday."

I felt bad when I told her it was actually Sunday. She looked at me with such embarrassment and shock.

"Oh no," she said. "I need to get back down town. I thought it was Saturday. Do you mind if I just sit here for a while until I figure out what to do?"

I told her no problem, and she sat at the table in the far corner. As I looked at her and the situation more carefully, I realized she must have been so poor, and maybe even homeless. She was dressed in the dingiest clothes that hadn't been washed in a while. She had a snug, winter hat on, three layers of flannel, baggy pants, worn-through tennis shoes, and gloves. Her gloves were turned inside out. They had fringes coming off all sides.

I felt right then and there that I should have made her a sandwich free of charge. Then I should talk to her, telling her that whatever she did, God loved her and wanted her to trust him and fall into his arms once again. I knew where all of this was coming from. I knew God was giving me these words and asking me to go talk to her. But what if . . . what if . . . the usual questions and doubts about why I shouldn't.

I went back to work, trying to forget about it, and hoping she would leave soon. My next customer came about an hour after that. She was a woman in her early thirties. She was well dressed in what looked like a work outfit. She had her hair pulled up nicely, and she was laced with perfume.

I made her some sandwiches, and we were at the cash register when she asked me how long the other woman had been sitting there. I told her about an hour.

"Did she get anything to eat?" the lady asked me.

I said no, and told her about the busses. Then the lady asked me if I wouldn't mind making one more sandwich. I looked at her and smiled.

I never made a sandwich with such happiness and at the same time guilt. I told the lady no charge, and handed her a bag of chips to go with it. She thanked me and then went to the other woman.

She handed her the food and began to talk to her. They must have talked for two hours before I saw them leave. As I was cleaning the tables and feeling bad for not talking to the woman myself, I noticed that she had left her gloves.

I told God that I was sorry for disobeying him. He told me something that will always give me a boldness in these situations, something that will never make me hesitate to tell others of him:

"You feel like she missed something because you lost your boldness, but she didn't lose her opportunity. The other woman is sharing with her right now and she will not lose out on me.

"You lost. You passed up the chance to gain something. You just let a wonderful flame go past you and into the hands of another. Let this be known, child, when you do not follow through with the boldness and knowledge I have given you, more than one person is affected by it. You are as well as they."

Acceptance Isn't Approval

Rachel had a way of feeling people's pain. But one thing that's important to understand is that while she welcomed and accepted everyone, she didn't necessarily approve of everything people did. This is a subtle but significant distinction that is key to being the kind of person who wants to create a chain reaction.

Rachel and I had many talks about the difference between acceptance and approval, and a lot of these talks revolved around my understanding of how a mother or father loves a child.

When parents love a child, that love endures even though the child can do a lot of things of which the parents do not approve. But parents should never reject their children simply because they do things of which they don't approve. I always wanted my children to feel acceptance from me, even at the same time they felt my disapproval of some of their actions. Disapproval should never dismiss people as people, but should relate only to people's actions, attitudes, and deeds.

Rachel understood that. As a result, she could be a close friend with someone who totally disagreed with her moral values and her ethics. All these things didn't have to line up 100 percent because she could connect with others on the level of human relationships.

Rachel didn't feel that friendship meant she had to accept everything. At the same time that she befriended people, she could confront them about the things she disagreed with. And since they knew she cared for them, they were able to handle that.

Too often, many of us pick and choose our friends based on approval rather than acceptance. We find people who think the way we do or agree with us. I believe we might find much more valuable and exciting friendships if we simply let people be the issue instead of what they believed or what they thought.

In the wake of the Columbine tragedy, I have had the opportunity to visit our nation's capital and testify before Congress. While there, I was startled to find out that some of those who sit on opposite ends of the Senate floor totally disagree on issues, argue and scream at each other, then go out and have lunch together and are closest friends. They are able to lay aside their political disagreements and enjoy being with each other as friends.

That was something Rachel was able to do. At times she really struggled with the temptation to give in to peer pressure. She even wrote about those struggles in her journal, where she described her efforts to resist those temptations to outwardly conform to what others were doing.

Rachel clearly understood the difference between acceptance and approval. She knew the value of being able to say, "I can accept you as a person without approving of everything you do." It's a lesson we all need to learn if we are going to develop welcoming hearts to the outsiders in our midst.

Love Versus Legalism

I want to say a few things here about some of the unique challenges that face religious people concerning this issue of acceptance.

It should come as no surprise to people who read *Rachel's Tears*, the earlier book about Rachel's life and death and the contents of her private journals, that Rachel was a Christian. She considered her faith in God the foundation of everything she did in life, including the ways she reached out to needy people around her.

That's why it often surprised Rachel that many other people who called themselves Christians seemed to be more judgmental of the outcasts in our world rather than more welcoming of them.

Rachel didn't fit the stereotypical mold of a religious person. I personally have resisted the pressure to conform to one mold of Christianity or to be labeled as one thing or the other. There is a form of judgment that is common in our country where we label people as a particular brand, causing them to lose their individuality and flavor. I saw Rachel develop that same way. She wanted to be a caring and loving individual, not a cloned representative of any particular church or creed.

We all know religious people who have molded themselves into a legalistic format of strict and inflexible rights and wrongs. For Rachel, her sense of right and wrong came from something deeper than external laws and regulations. Her ethics were based on internal convictions about good and evil rather than legalism.

Rachel and I often talked about the fact that legalism doesn't change people's hearts. I was raised in legalism, and I learned at an early age that all the rules in the world didn't change my heart and my desires to do things I knew were harmful or wrong.

I have also done some research into the Puritans, those God-fearing people who came to America from Europe to have religious freedom and then turned around and became so cruel to others who believed differently that they would torture and kill those they labeled as witches without much evidence of real witchcraft. On the surface, the Puritans seemed to be good people, and I believe in their hearts they were good people. But their emphasis on legalism sometimes outweighed their obligation to love other people.

I think it's fascinating that when Jesus walked this earth, the people who were attracted to Him were the outcasts and the sinners, while the religious legalists sought to put Him to death. He broke all those rules. When His disciples were hungry, He allowed them to harvest and eat corn on the Sabbath, saying that there were weightier matters of justice and mercy than a strict legalistic observance of religious rules.

Our Need for Rules

Don't get me wrong. I think rules are important. The law is the law. Rules are there to teach us and guide us into right behavior. But rules don't make us honest and pure people. That comes from inside. Rules provide the form, but the spiritual and ethical formation comes from within.

If I lived all by myself like Tom Hanks in the movie *Cast Away,* I wouldn't need lots of rules to organize society on my solitary island. But anytime you have more than one person involved in any activity, there have to be boundaries—or rules and regulations. Rules and regulations are there primarily to prevent us from taking advantage of each other or misusing each other.

There are things that are deeper than man-made rules. These are the universal principles such as mercy, kindness, and forgiveness and reaching out to others. These are the kinds of things that all religions and many philosophies all over the world teach in common. These are the rules that you can't really put in a rulebook. How can you delegate or administer mercy? How can you punish someone for not showing acceptance? How can you condense into a formula the concept of forgiveness?

These are the intangibles that make life possible in a complex society like ours, and they were principles that Rachel tried to put into action at Columbine High School.

Creating a Welcoming Environment

So how do we behave in such a way that we create an environment that makes outcasts and other fringe kids feel as if they are welcomed and accepted?

It is a complex question, but recently I came across an article that dealt with just this issue. The article was entitled "Reaching Everyday Outcasts: How to Build a Group Environment That Welcomes, Nurtures, and Challenges the 'Faceless Fringe Kids' in Your Community." "The startling common thread among the teenagers who have planned and carried out deadly assaults on their classmates over the last few years is that they've all been 'average' kids who were force-fed a steady diet of bullying, taunting, and exclusion," begins the article. "They were everyday outcasts. And your community is full of everyday outcasts. The key question: Is your group the kind of place where outcasts can feel safe, nurtured, and challenged?"

Scott Larson, who runs a church-based outreach to troubled kids in Massachusetts, wrote the article. It appeared in the July-August 2000 issue of *Group Magazine*.

I'm including much of this lengthy article in this chapter because I think it speaks so clearly to the things Rachel was trying to do in her own life. And even though both the article and the magazine in which it appeared are intended to be read primarily by people who lead religious youth groups, I think the principles in the article can help schoolteachers, guidance counselors, and young people who are trying to reach out to the needy people we see all around us every day.

Three Danger Signs

The problem with so many young people growing up in our culture is that they lack both healthy adult relationships and healthy peer relationships. These kids are susceptible to three damaging trajectories:

1. They become loners who feel like they don't fit in anywhere. As one young man so pointedly said to me, "To be an outcast is to be a nonperson."

2. They bond to negative peers who'll offer them what they crave—acceptance. Children who lack positive relationships with adults are prone to form destructive connections as they seek peers with similar problems. Luke Woodham, the sixteen-year-old who murdered three students in Pearl, Mississippi, told ABC News that he felt isolated and rejected in his community. Thus, he was easily drawn into a group of boys who were self-proclaimed Satanists.

3. They become prey for unhealthy adults with ulterior motives. Dangerous cults and groups that profit from the sexual exploitation of young people actively recruit outcasts because they know how easily they can be enticed.

If you know teenagers who are hurtling along on one of these destructive trajectories, they're at great risk of inflicting harm on themselves or others. Void of healthy outside perspectives, their world is wrapped in the pain of the present. Unable to visualize how things could possibly change for the better, they feel trapped and hopeless.

Peers Can Help

While adult intervention is the key to reaching traditional at-risk young people, peers are the keys to reaching ostracized and bullied kids. There are so many of these kids that there's no way adult staffers can reach them all. And most of us don't have the same access to outcast kids as our teenagers do. Just as vicious peer-to-peer interactions can send ostracized kids over the edge, grace-full interactions can build a new sense of worth and self-respect in them.

One seventeen-year-old girl understood this reality and expressed it eloquently in a recent letter to the editor in *Newsweek* magazine:

> To all my fellow students who may be reading this: You could prevent another tragedy from happening in your own seemingly safe school. Say hello to the guy who sits alone in chemistry and never speaks. Invite someone who always sits by herself at lunch to sit with you.
>
> Think about what you are doing when you tease, laugh at, or exclude someone from something just because he doesn't fit in. This may not solve the problem; some people are just not mentally stable. But if the youth in our schools make an effort to stop ostracizing such students, schools might become safer places. Maybe even happier too.

Larson writes that kids know they belong to a group when a peer invites them to come, when others in the group embrace them, and when they're given opportunities to lead and contribute to the group.

A Strategy for Welcoming the Outcasts

Reaching out to outcasts and welcoming them into our groups is not always easy. That's why Larson writes at length about developing a strategy for integrating fringe kids. That strategy involves at least three steps:

1. **Establishing genuine love.** You cannot expect your teenagers to embrace outcasts if they have not yet learned to love themselves. The second greatest Commandment says, "Love your neighbor as yourself." Because of insecurity, many kids detest or hate themselves, making it impossible for them to effectively reach out to their neighbors.

Tabatha was always more comfortable in the predictable world of adults. She was unprepared for the severe bullying she endured in eighth grade. She was frequently roughed up in the halls by other girls and called dirty names on a daily basis.

During that year she latched onto the gothic lifestyle as a way to deal with her increasing estrangement from peers. Her melancholy rapidly shifted to rage. She began to fight back when teased or ridiculed and frequently was sent to the principal's office.

Early in her ninth-grade year, she got into a knockdown, drag-out fight with four of her tormentors at a shopping mall. Her parents talked to school officials about the problem. Tabatha told her therapist that she was constantly afraid at school, had no friends, and was thoroughly miserable. "Maybe the world would be better off without me," she concluded.

Not knowing what else to do, Tabatha's parents urged her to join a local youth group. They persuaded her that this would give her a chance to meet more positive young people.

"The church group was more depressing than school was because I expected more from it," said Tabatha. Her youth group peers also made fun of her appearance. Right in front of the youth director, teenagers leaned away from her and made faces, rolling their eyes whenever she ventured an opinion during Bible study.

"Knowing that even people who called themselves Christians rejected me made me feel worse than ever," said Tabatha. "But I suppose most of them weren't really there for God anyway. They were probably forced to attend, like me."

2. **The power of events.** Use big events to introduce outcast kids to the group. It can be intimidating for everyone involved when fringe kids are introduced into a youth group meeting. It is threatening for the youth group kids because outsiders are treading on their safe and predictable turf, and intimidating for the fringe kids because they can quickly discern when they are unwelcome.

Inviting new kids to special events allows both "insiders" and "outsiders" to come together on common ground and bond through their shared experience. Also, these activities typically offer an extended time for new relationships to form and deepen. When kids return to the regular youth group setting, they are maintaining momentum rather than trying to forge new relationships.

Dave was quiet, shy, overweight, and the butt of countless jokes. Away from the crowds he had a keen sense of humor and was quite talented and creative. But few ever tasted these good things because he had learned to survive by avoiding the spotlight. For Dave, attention was always closely linked to humiliation.

One of my staffers, John, led a group of kids including Dave on a mission trip to Jamaica a few years ago. "A whole new Dave emerged in Jamaica," recalls John. "Some of the groups that had arrived from different parts of the United States were having difficulty gelling. Dave arose as sort of the 'MC' of the whole group. Everyone saw him as the fun, caring kid with the Boston accent—not as the fat, quiet kid everyone made fun of. The transformation was incredible.

"When Dave wasn't around, others would look for him. A hard worker and a soother of the hurting, he was also shedding the chains that had so tightly bound him. He even got up to participate in the talent show the last night.

"When we got back, everyone was amazed when Dave got up in front of the youth group to share his experiences. For the first time, they were laughing with him and not at him. He still got teased after that, but he was able to put up with it and to stick up for himself when he needed to. But he never retreated into his cocoon."

What fueled the change? Peer acceptance, important responsibilities, and a safe environment. And when others saw who he really was, instead of who he wasn't, they liked him. Outside the group's normal environment, other group members could see what was there all along.

3. **Clear rules.** Establish clear rules and boundaries at youth group events. Unclear expectations can derail fringe kids who are trying to integrate into the group. The regulars want things to stay as they've always been, but new kids have no idea what that means. They need to know the group's standards, and the "regulars" need to know bullying won't be tolerated.

One of the best bullying prevention techniques is to talk frankly with your kids. First, ask them to define what acts constitute bullying. As they come up with things such as gossiping, mocking, public humiliation, name-calling, dirty looks, and exclusion, ask how many have experienced these things in the past year. Then ask how big a problem they think bullying is in your youth group.

Once you all agree on the problem, invite suggestions about what the group can do to prevent these harmful acts in the future. As they take ownership of both the problem and the solution, they will be more committed to stopping harmful actions.

Mike, a local youth leader, told me how one of his kids, Brian, was always picking on younger, smaller kids in the group. Mike confronted Brian on numerous occasions, but nothing changed. He even spoke to Brian's parents and threatened to kick him out of the group.

When sign-up time came for the fall youth retreat, Brian's name was at the top of the list. "We can't let him go or I'll be chasing him all weekend," was Mike's first thought. But after praying about it, he didn't feel it would be right to ban Brian from the retreat. Instead, on the opening night, he clearly laid out the ground rules for the weekend, including mistreatment of others.

As Mike explained that everyone was responsible for the climate of the group, kids seemed to understand. He asked for their input on what behaviors constituted bullying and invited ideas on how it should be addressed. Later that evening, when Brian started picking on someone, his friends stepped in to confront him.

"You're turning my friends against me!" charged Brian, as he angrily confronted Mike later that evening. Mike again explained why his actions were unacceptable and why nobody in the youth group would tolerate them. "If somebody picks on you, we would be there in your defense as well," he said.

The next evening, a frustrated Brian finally broke down in tears. He confessed that he'd been brutalized by an older brother all his life. He assumed bullying was the only way he could feel good about himself.

From time to time, Brian would sink back into old patterns, but each time his peers would either say something or simply give him a disapproving look. That was all it took for him to stop. The youth group helped Brian break a pattern he had been entrenched in since childhood. Much to his surprise, the group didn't reject him for his actions, but embraced him through loving confrontation.

Effective bullying prevention strategies require that group leaders start early. Bullying behavior begins as soon as young people sense the differences between themselves and their peers. Older teenagers can have a huge impact on the bullying behavior of children. Because children look to teenagers to learn acceptable patterns of behavior, teenagers are in a unique position to give instruction, especially regarding respectful peer relationships.

Have your group members plan an anti-bullying presentation for their classes (first through eighth grades) using skits, puppets, or stories. As your kids teach, they will more deeply own their convictions.

(Reprinted with permission, *Group Magazine*, copyright 2000, Group Publishing, Inc., Box 481, Loveland, CO 80539.)

Developing a Caring Lifestyle

Love isn't worth much if it's just a feeling that is never expressed, and mercy is little more than sentiment if it isn't shown to the people who need it most.

Love and mercy can become powerful tools to heal our world if we apply them with consistency and compassion toward the people around us who need them most.

It isn't always easy thinking about other people and their needs, but if we develop a lifestyle of caring and compassion, it becomes easier. I will talk about this lifestyle in the next chapter.

12
Walking the Path of Kindness

Ours is a fast-paced world full of people busily moving from one place to another in a mad scramble for survival and happiness. But while we all have to play a part in the so-called rat race, I would like to challenge you to begin walking a different path, the path of kindness.

The rules of the rat race dictate that every rat looks out for himself. The path of kindness requires something entirely different: that we look out for the needs of others around us.

Victory in the rat race is determined by which rat finishes ahead of all the other rats and has the most cheese to eat. Success on the path of kindness is much harder to judge, but is based on how one has invested his life in the lives of others.

In the rat race, everything is focused on me, me, me. But on the path of kindness, one sees that this is a very large planet full of billions of unique and valuable people, each of them deserving of love and compassion.

Frankly, most people think the rat race is good enough. After all, folks seem to get along pretty well most of the time.

Then something like Columbine happens, and everyone asks how something so horrible could happen. Such tragedies force us all to evaluate our world and the way we live our lives and hopefully result in finding an approach that is healthier and happier.

In this chapter, I am going to ask you to consider leaving the rat race to begin walking the path of kindness. If you are interested in living your life for something bigger than yourself and your own wants and needs, keep reading and you will see how you can start a chain reaction of kindness that spreads its goodness to everyone else you come in contact with.

From Random Kindness to Intentional Goodness

In 1993, the editors at Conari Press, a small publisher in Berkeley, California, published a little book called *Random Acts of Kindness*. The book was full of stories and practical suggestions from dozens of people who had devoted part of their lives to making the world a better place for everyone.

That small book, which helped a small but devoted kindness movement grow into a national trend, began with this introduction:

Random acts of kindness are those little sweet or grand lovely things we do for no reason except that, momentarily, the best of our humanity has sprung, exquisitely, into full bloom.

When you spontaneously give an old woman the bouquet of red carnations you had meant to take home to your own dinner table, when you give your lunch to the guitar-playing beggar who makes music at the corner between your two subway stops, when you anonymously put coins in someone else's parking meter because you see the red "Expired" medallion signaling to a meter maid—you are doing not what life requires of you, but what the best of your human soul invites you to do.

Most of us try hard to fulfill our obligations in life, to be responsible parents, to reward and discipline our children, to assist our employees or colleagues, to support and comfort our spouses, to do our share of the work at the office and at home. But these deeds are what we're expected to do, what in fact we have agreed to do because of the mates we have chosen, the lives we have decided to live. They come, in effect, with the territory. To be responsible, decent, civilized human beings who maintain the stability of our lives and our relationships, we must and we will do all these ordinary things.

But it is when we step outside the arena of our normal circumstances, when we move beyond the familiar emotional and circumstantial boundaries of our lives that our kindnesses, too, move beyond the routine and enter the realm of the extraordinary and exquisite. Instead of being responsible good deeds they become embodiments of compassion.

To become the perpetrator of random acts of kindness, then, is to become in some sense an angel. For it means you have moved beyond the limits of your daily human condition to touch wings with the divine.

As far as I know, Rachel never read this book. But these words could have been her mission statement for life. The only difference with Rachel was that for her, kindness was not random at all. It was a way of life. It was a path she walked every day.

Rachel made a decision to live her life in such a way that she would be a source of kindness that would cause a ripple effect that would continue to touch others.

As I travel around the country and speak to groups about

Columbine and Rachel's values, I find many people who seem hungry to live better, fuller, and more productive lives. I believe walking the path of kindness is a powerful way to do these things.

A Long Journey Starts with Small Steps

If I am going to walk from Denver to Dallas, I better be in good shape and have some good walking shoes. It would also be helpful to have a good map, some sunglasses, and a raincoat.

But all the preparations in the world can't get me from here to there unless I do one simple thing: put one foot in front of the other and start walking. The progress will be slow, but if I put my mind (and my legs) to it, I can make progress in the journey.

Likewise, walking the path of kindness starts with small steps. I don't have to begin by ridding the world of crime and pain. Rather, I can begin right where I am by helping the people around me who are suffering.

Anyone can start taking initial steps on the path of kindness by doing small, simple things. At least that is the theory behind a recent book called *Say Please, Say Thank You: The Respect We Owe Each Other*.

Author Donald McCullough says, "Life is filled with little opportunities to make a difference. Sometimes it's as simple as saying please or thank you, keeping a secret, or treating elders with respect."

These things may seem small and insignificant, but think how different our world would be if everyone practiced these basic techniques of kindness.

On a much bigger scale, there are worldwide efforts like Make a Difference Day, which celebrated its tenth anniversary in October 2000. An article in the October 20-22 issue of *USA Weekend* featured an advance look at some of the activities an expected two million volunteers were planning to participate in during this incredible day of community service:

> From the slopes of a volcanic crater in Hawaii to a teen center near Times Square, from a suburban London hospital to the streets of Tel Aviv, the tenth Make a Difference Day promises to be bigger and better than ever.
>
> Some of the volunteer projects are pure brawn: In Hawaii, soldiers from the Army's 25th Infantry will rappel down the razor-edge slopes of Diamond Head's volcanic crater to remove trash.
>
> Others are pure heart: Ida Perez, ten, of Lubbock, Texas, has terminal brain cancer and will be lavished with love all day by a dozen "adopted" moms, members of the Catholic Daughters of the Americas. While they care for Ida, her true mother will spend the day rejuvenating for tougher times ahead.
>
> In Abilene, Texas, 50,000 will tackle a wide range of community projects.
>
> In Louisville, 50,000 Future Farmers of America teenagers attending their convention will join with USA Harvest to fight hunger by collecting 70,000 cans of food.
>
> At the state level, all 50 governors have declared their support for Make a Difference Day.
>
> In Israel, trees will be planted in a low-income Tel Aviv neighborhood on Sunday, October 29, the alternate date for those with religious conflicts on Saturday.
>
> In the United Kingdom's fifth Make a Difference Day, 26,000 people are expected in 1,200 projects. Sidcup, a London suburb, will collect aluminum cans to raise money for children's cancer (and perhaps win a Guinness Book of Records title for longest string of cans).

In Brazil, college Students in Free Enterprise hope to lead one million volunteers in 30,000 projects.

In 150 cities including Sydney, Moscow, and Shanghai, 15,000 Chase Manhattan workers, family and friends will volunteer in Global Days of Service.

Justin Timberlake of the popular singing group 'N Sync was one of the event's many celebrity participants. "The slightest effort can make the biggest difference in someone's life," said the eighteen-year-old Memphis native who regularly meets with critically ill kids from the Make a Wish Foundation.

"I was raised up in a Southern home where you learn that you help your neighbor," he explains. "This is something I feel is more important than anything else: If you can help somebody, why not?"

The key to helping, for Justin, is finding causes he enjoys. "I have a thing for little kids," he admits with his slow smile. "I see kids and I just want to help them." Then, too, "music is also something I enjoy. I want to show people how special it can be. People can make a big difference with things close to their heart." Justin wants his school programs to give kids a creative outlet and expand their horizons. "Studies have shown that kids who learn music do better in math, better in spelling. Give these kids training, next thing you know they start a garage band and become Pearl Jam."

He wants to touch individual kids with his good deeds but his real goal is grander: "I want to reach the world." In fact, with regard to the Make a Difference Day, he said he hoped everyone would "go for it." "Seeing a smile on a kid's face and knowing you put it there is the best feeling in the world. It makes you feel better about yourself, about everything." It makes a difference.

(For more information about this annual event, visit the organization's Web site at Makeadifferenceday.com. The site can be searched by zip code or key word so you can find activities in your region or area of interest.)

How Do You Want to Be Remembered?

On April 24, 1999, nearly three thousand people crowded into Littleton's Trinity Christian Center for Rachel Scott's funeral, an event that was broadcast around the world by CNN.

I'll never forget all the people who spoke at Rachel's funeral and all of the wonderful things they said. I want to include some of their comments here, not to make Rachel seem larger than life but to demonstrate that a life of compassion and kindness can create a powerful ripple effect that touches many lives.

Lori Johnson was Rachel's youth pastor. She knew Rachel well:

What I wanted to say about Rachel was that she was an amazing, amazing girl. She had this fun, full-of-life side where she had so much energy and made people laugh. She would wear these crazy hats sometimes, and dress in crazy ways just to be different. She was never afraid of being her own person. That's what she wanted to be, and I always admired the strength that she had.

She also had this really deep thoughtful side. She would write poetry, and she cared so much about people. Through it all, there was a passion and a love that she had for God and for people that consumed her life and consumed everything about her.

Mark Bodiford was a young man in the youth group whom Rachel reached out to and befriended:

I haven't had the best life, and I've always prayed to God that he would send somebody who would love me, who would care about me, and who would make me feel wanted. I just praise God for sending me an angel. In the short time that we had our friendship, Rachel made me feel like the most important person in this world. She called me her bigger brother, and I just say this to you, Rachel: I love you, and I know you're in heaven, and I'll see you there someday.

Nick Baumgart took Rachel to the Columbine prom the Tuesday before the shootings:

Rachel was my friend, and a truer friend you couldn't find. Her name, Rachel Joy Scott, is perfect right in the middle there. Joy was what she brought to everybody she ever met. Whether you knew her or not, it didn't matter, she still brought it to you.

Also, her trueness to herself was amazing. She didn't let anybody affect who she was. She didn't let anybody tell her that what she believed and who she was wasn't okay. She was true to herself, and because of that, she was true to everybody else.

In a sense, she still is here. She always will be, and that smile will always be here. You know, you could be having the worst day of your entire life and all she had to do was smile. I'm lucky to have known her, I'm fortunate to have been her friend, and I'm fortunate to have called her my prom date. But I'm truly blessed to have had her in my life.

Sergio Gonzales had been a friend of Rachel's since the fourth grade:

We met the first day of class, and she shined back then too. Here's just one quick story.

I remember one Halloween. I wore a Zorro costume to school, and I hated it because my mom made it and I felt pretty dorky. And Rachel came to me and said, "What's wrong with you, Serge? I love Zorro. I like him. I'd like to be him. You wanna switch costumes with me?" And ever since then, we just had this bond that grew and grew ever since our first play in fourth grade and until our last play that we just performed at Columbine.

I know Rachel loved life because life was just like one big amusement park to Rachel, and a glorification to God. She always told me to love life and not worry so much about the little things. She was the kind of person who would tell me, "Serge, you need to get over it." She taught me that more than anybody else, and I'll always remember her.

Brianna Cook was someone Rachel reached out to at school:

What I remember most about Rachel is when I first came to Columbine, I didn't fit in or anything, and Rachel was the first person who ever came up to me and opened her heart to me and brought me in.

My car always died and we'd always go to Subway to find Rachel and she'd always jump my car. It was the little things like that always meant a lot to me, and she always put her feelings aside and put other people's feelings up front. She wrote me a lot of poetry that means a lot to me. I love her.

Andrew Robinson was assigned to be Rachel's mentor in forensics and drama. He wrote the play that Rachel starred in weeks before the shooting:

My name is Andrew Robinson, but to Rachel I was just Robinson. I was assigned to her early on to be her mentor. Pretty much everybody who had me as a mentor wanted to be reassigned, because I have kind of a reputation for not being very nice, I guess. On the first day, when I told her she could be reassigned to someone else if she acted quickly, she looked at me and said, "I can take anything you can dish out and then some. So bring it." And I said, "Okay, we're going to bring it."

I've never met a finer young woman with such drive and goals, and I always thought that when I left Columbine it was in good hands because she was right there keeping step with me. I really thank her for that. She reaffirmed my belief that there really are truly truly truly good people.

Sarah Scott was one of Rachel's cousins and a close friend. Rachel had written some kind words in Sarah's school yearbook:

One thing she wrote to me was: "Don't let your character change color with your environment. Find who you are and let it stay in its true colors."

The night she died, I wrote a poem about her. It's called "Angel of Mine."

> Looking down, seeing despair
> Only leaving a soul searching for air
> Feeling the warmth, seeing the light

Reaching for wings for the eternal flight
Slipping away from this world today
Angel of mine you've found your way.
Let my love be the wind beneath your wing
As you rejoice in heaven and sing.
Angel of mine
Your face will make the heavens so bright
With your beauty, grace, and loving spirit.

If you were to die today, how would people remember you? How many people would stand up and speak about the good deeds you had done?

Think for a moment about your life and how you live it. Perhaps you will be inspired to begin living more for others than for yourself by showing kindness whenever you can.

Kindness Is Good for You

You don't have to be gone for kindness to begin having an impact on your life. More and more, medical science is proving that a life full of kindness reaps immediate rewards in terms of greater health and happiness.

Barry K. Weinhold works at the University of Colorado at Colorado Springs where he has established an organization called the Kindness Campaign. Among other things, the Kindness Campaign has published a manual called *Spreading Kindness: A Program Guide for Reducing Youth and Peer Violence in the Schools*. (For information, visit the www.uccs.edu/~kindness Web site.)

Weinhold believes that kindness is not only good for those who are on the receiving end, but he has also compiled research that shows the benefits of kindness to those who show it. He describes some of these benefits in an article titled "Being Kind Is Good for Your Health."

While medical researchers have searched in vain for years to find a cure for the common cold, new medical research shows that being kind can have powerful healing effects on illnesses such as colds, flu or stress-related illnesses. Researchers who are from a new field of medicine, called psychoneuroimmuniology, have found that kind thoughts, words and deeds can help us stay healthy.

These researchers have found that even kind thoughts can have a positive effect on the body's immune system, our first line of defense against disease. They discovered that our immunological resistance to the common cold is significantly increased when we do kind acts to help other people.

There is mounting evidence that thinking about and doing kind acts produce health benefits very similar to those achieved from exercise programs.

For example, people who regularly are kind and helpful to others develop stronger immune systems, improve their cardiovascular circulation, enjoy a heightened sense of well-being and even live longer. They found that as little as two hours per week, or seventeen minutes per day of kind acts, can produce the significant health gains mentioned above.

Why and how this works is explained by researcher Paul Persall who tells us that when we help others, our brain releases endorphins (en-dor' fins), which are morphine-like chemicals that give us the same feelings of exhilaration that joggers call the "runner's high." He also discovered that when you are kind, your brain releases another chemical that inhibits the release of what he called "Substance P," a neurotransmitter chemical that communicates pain messages to the brain.

Other researchers have found that the reverse is true as well. They found that when you are angry with others, the flow of the helpful endorphins is cut off by adrenaline that supports fight, flight or freeze behaviors. This was found to lower immune functioning and limit any of the possible health benefits of being kind.

Weinhold summarized the many physiological and psychological benefits that can result from being kind, saying that they included these potential results:

> Strengthens the immune system
> Reduces physical pain
> Produces feelings of exhilaration
> Increases body warmth
> Develops a sense of joy
> Improves weight control
> Heightens sense of well-being
> Reduces sleeplessness
> Increases happiness
> Improves circulation
> Promotes optimism
> Leads to fewer colds
> Generates sense of calmness
> Causes drop in blood pressure
> Provides more energy
> Improves cardiovascular functioning
> Enhances relaxation

Reduces stomach acid

Improves sense of connectedness

Slows progress of cancer

Reminds us of spiritual connections

Decreases oxygen consumption

Decreases loneliness

Relieves arthritis symptoms

Decreases hostility

Relieves lupus symptoms

Decreases depression

Relieves asthma symptoms

Decreases feelings of helplessness

Increases longevity

"These benefits are available to all of us, if we choose to think and act in kind ways toward ourselves and others," says Weinhold. "We can choose to exercise our 'kindness muscles' and live a healthier, more enjoyable and longer life or we can choose to exercise our 'violence muscles' and live a less healthy, less enjoyable and shorter life. The choice is yours. I know what I am going to choose."

Try It for Thirty Days; You'll Like It!

Just as my walk from Denver to Dallas begins with one small step at a time, you might need to start with some small steps as you're making the transition from the rat race to the path of kindness.

It has been said that if something is repeated enough times it becomes a habit. Habits are not easily formed, and sometimes they are even difficult and uncomfortable to form at first. Initially, a new habit may not seem natural, but eventually, if you do something over and over again, it becomes a habit. Once this happens, it's easier to do it than not to do it. It becomes second nature, a basic part of your life.

There are some people in the world who seem to be unusually gifted with an ability to be compassionate and kind. Rachel was one of those people. I think most people are more like me—we have to work at it.

For many people, life seemed happy enough running the rat race, but at some point in their lives, something happened to trigger them into a different attitude and they began practicing repetitive acts of kindness and forming a new kind of habit. For some people I know, Columbine was the triggering event. Once their new kindness habit was formed, it was effortless and natural for them.

How many repetitions of an act does it take to form a habit? No one can be sure. I think thirty times might be a good start.

I want to challenge you to give your new life a chance. For thirty days be on the lookout for ways that you can do simple acts of kindness to other people. At the end of the month, if you have consciously chosen to show compassion and love and kindness to others, it just might become a lifetime habit.

You can't change the world in thirty days, but you just might change yourself, and in the process, you'll be making the world a better place to live, not only for yourself but also for all those whose lives you touch.

Go, my friend, and in the words of Rachel Scott, START A CHAIN REACTION!

About the Author

Darrell Scott has become a crusader since his daughter's death in the Columbine High School tragedy. Darrell Scott has spoken to millions of people in schools, universities, churches, civic auditoriums, and coliseums all over the world, challenging his listeners to follow Rachel's example of practical compassion. He is the founder of The Columbine Redemption, and he has testified before the U.S. Congress on the issue of school violence. He is the co-author of the best-selling book *Rachel's Tears*.

For information on speaking engagements go to

www.rachelscott.com or www.ambassadoragency.com.

Also from Darrell Scott

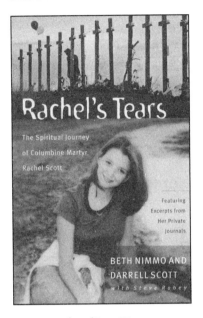

Rachel's Tears
The Spiritual Journey of
Columbine Martyr Rachel Scott

By Beth Nimmo and Darrell Scott with Steve Rabey

Rachel Scott was a typical teenage girl who was incredibly dedicated to following and serving Christ. Though she was mocked for her beliefs, at times doubted her faith, and constantly struggled with personal issues every teenager faces, she remained faithful to God. Then on April 20, 1999, at Columbine High School, she was killed for that faith.

The bestselling book *Rachel's Tears* is a moving meditation on the life, death, and faith of Rachel as seen through the eyes of her parents and through writings and drawings from her journals. Her parents also offer a spiritual perspective on the Columbine tragedy and provide a vision for preventing youth violence across the nation.

ISBN 0-7852-6848-0